"鲁班工坊"工程实践创新项目（EPIP）系列教材

"Luban Workshop" Engineering Practice Innovation Project（EPIP） Textbook Series

VBSE Integrating with Modern International Market Environment

VBSE 融合现代国际市场环境

徐　文　胡杰林　编著

Xu Wen　Hu Jielin

蒋晓燕　主审

Jiang Xiaoyan

天津大学出版社

TIANJIN UNIVERSITY PRESS

图书在版编目(CIP)数据

VBSE融合现代国际市场环境 / 徐文, 胡杰林编著.
— 天津 : 天津大学出版社, 2018.5
（“鲁班工坊”工程实践创新项目（EPIP）系列教材）
ISBN 978-7-5618-6127-1

Ⅰ. ①V… Ⅱ. ①徐… ②胡… Ⅲ. ①企业经营管理－应用软件 Ⅳ. ①F270.7

中国版本图书馆CIP数据核字(2018)第103017号

VBSE Ronghe Xiandai Guoji Shichang Huanjing

出版发行　天津大学出版社
地　　址　天津市卫津路92号天津大学内(邮编:300072)
电　　话　发行部:022-27403647
网　　址　publish.tju.edu.cn
印　　刷　廊坊市海涛印刷有限公司
经　　销　全国各地新华书店
开　　本　185mm×260mm
印　　张　11.25
字　　数　260千
版　　次　2018年5月第1版
印　　次　2018年5月第1次
定　　价　35.00元

“鲁班工坊”教材编审委员会

Editorial Committee of “Luban Workshop” Textbooks

序

用虚拟现实技术推动国际教育发展

“一带一路倡议”是世纪性的系统工程，不仅标志着中国国家发展战略和外交战略新的开端，而且为中国教育如何改革、国际教育如何发展提出了新命题。教育部在印发的《推进共建“一带一路”教育行动》中提出：“教育为国家富强、民族繁荣、人民幸福之本，在共建‘一带一路’中具有基础性和先导性作用。教育交流为沿线各国民心相通架设桥梁，人才培养为沿线各国政策沟通、设施联通、贸易畅通、资金融通提供支撑。”天津市作为国家现代职业教育改革创新示范区，从2016年开始在“一带一路”沿线国家搭建“鲁班工坊”平台，把优秀职业教育成果输出国门与世界分享，成为“一带一路”上的技术“驿站”。

科技助力教育变革，创新推动教育发展。作为教育型企业，我们希望通过先进技术的应用改变教学和学习场景。此次与天津渤海职业技术学院联合推出“鲁班工坊”系列教材，就是希望通过产教融合把创新的协同育人模式与“一带一路倡议”相连接，促进国际教育繁荣。

虚拟现实被认为是21世纪重要的发展学科以及影响人们生活的重要技术之一，新道科技股份有限公司率先将VR/AR技术融入商科实践教学，通过软硬件结合，首创ARE人机交互“场景式教学”平台，在教学方法、教学内容和教学环境上实现了重大突破，践行了用技术引领中国实践教学发展、服务中国教育事业的使命。

在这个平台上，教师可以进行企业情境构建和业务仿真案例解析，学生可以身临其境地体验到与现实中多种行业一样的工作情境。这种教学模式最大的特点表现在三个方面：一是解决了商科实践教学的可视化难题；二是通过全脑学习，培养学生的全局观和系统思维；三是形成多感官刺激、多维度视听感受，大大激发了学生的学习动机，增强了其学习的情境感和沉浸感。这种“虚拟现实场景+真实业务内容”的混合模式，在培养学生的全局观和系统思维的同时，也提高了学生就业后的岗位适应力和胜任力。这种模式可帮助院校学生实现情境化学习、协作式学习、自主性学习、探究式学习、对抗性学习等各种形式的学习实践活动。此种教学模式既是商科类的“工程实践创新”，又是对商科专业实践课程改革的一次尝试，具有极其重要的意义。

“鲁班工坊”系列教材出版，既是现代职业教育体系建设与创新的重大举措，也是积极响应并服务国家“一带一路倡议”的具体行动。同时，我非常高兴，此教材将会通过“鲁班工坊”平台提供给国际合作的外国学生使用，让 ARE 实践教学平台“走出去”，服务国际教育！

新技术、新应用、新场景，相信随着 ARE 实践教学平台在中国和“一带一路”沿线国家院校教育的应用和普及，必将推进“一带一路”国际教育的共同繁荣。作为教育型企业，我们愿意在力所能及的范围内承担更多责任、义务，为区域教育及国际教育大发展做出贡献！

新道科技股份有限公司董事长　郭延生

Promotion of International Education Development with Virtual Reality Technique

"The Belt and Road Initiative" is a great system engineering, which not only represents the new chapter of China's national development strategy and diplomatic strategy, but also puts forward a new proposition for Chinese education reform and international education development. Promoting the Education Co-construction Action for "the Belt and Road" issued by the Ministry of Education of the People's Republic of China mentioned, "Education is vital to the powerfulness of a country, the prosperity of all the nationalities and the happiness of people. It plays a fundamental and guiding role in the co-construction of 'the Belt and Road'. Educational exchange can serve as a bridge for close people-to-people ties, and talent cultivation can provide support for the countries along the route on policy coordination, connectivity of infrastructure, unimpeded trade, and financial integration." Tianjin, as a modern vocational education reform and innovation demonstration zone, has been building the platform of "Luban Workshop" in the countries along "the Belt and Road" since 2016. Tianjin shares the excellent vocational education results with the world and becomes a technical "post" along "the Belt and Road".

Science and technology offers help for education revolution, and innovation promotes educational development. As an educational enterprise, we hope to apply advanced technology to change teaching and learning scenes. Seentao Technology Co., Ltd. and Tianjin Bohai Vocational Technical College jointly launch the "Luban Workshop" textbook series to connect the cooperative education mode with "the Belt and Road Initiative" by industry-education integration to promote the prosperity of international education.

Virtual Reality (VR) is one of the hottest emerging technologies in the 21st century. Seentao Technology Co., Ltd. applies VR/AR into business practice teaching to create a new platform, which is ARE human–computer interaction teaching platform. Seentao has made great breakthroughs in teaching method, teaching content and teaching environment. The mission of Seentao is to provide services for the cause of Chinese education and guide Chinese practice teaching development by technology.

On this platform, lecturers can build enterprise situations and analyze virtual cases; students can experience virtual work environments. This teaching mode has three characteristics: first, it solves the problems of visualization of business practice teaching; second, it cultivates students' holistic view and systematic thinking; third, ARE can stimulate students' learning motivation by means of the technology of multi–sensory stimulation and multi–dimensional audio and visual experience. This mixed mode is "virtual enterprise situation + real business process", which is good for cultivating students' holistic view and systematic thinking. In addition, it can improve students' adaptive capacity and competency after graduation. Also, ARE can help students to learn, such as situational learning, collaborative learning, independent learning, explorative learning, and adversarial learning. ARE teaching mode is not only the "Engineering Practice Innovation" in business studies, but also a trial in business practice course reform. It is critical to business teaching.

The publishing of "Luban Workshop" textbook series is a great event of modern vocational education system's construction and innovation. At the same time, it is a specific action to actively respond to and serve "the Belt and Road Initiative". Meanwhile, I am very glad that the textbook will be provided for international students via "Luban Workshop" and ARE practice teaching platform will "go outside" to serve international education.

New technology, new application, and new scene, we believe , with ARE practice teaching platform's application and popularization in college education of China and the countries along "the Belt and Road", will promote the co–prosperity of international education along "the Belt and Road". As an educational enterprise, we are willing to take as many responsibilities and obligations as possible, and to make contributions to the great development of regional and international education.

GUO Yansheng

President of Seentao Technology Co., Ltd.

Contents

Chapter One Course Description ······ 1

Section One: Course Background ······ 2

1.1.1 Virtual Business Social Environment (VBSE) ······ 2

1.1.2 Augmented Reality Education (ARE) ······ 3

Section Two: Manufacturing Business Process ······ 5

1.2.1 Warehousing Process ······ 5

1.2.2 Production Process ······ 11

1.2.3 Equipment Rules ······ 12

1.2.4 Capacity Rules ······ 13

1.2.5 Process Route ······ 14

1.2.6 Procurement Process ······ 16

1.2.7 Sales Process ······ 17

1.2.8 Market Development Process ······ 17

1.2.9 Financial Process ······ 18

1.2.10 Human Resources Process ······ 22

1.2.11 Logistics Process ······ 25

Section Three: System Operation Training ······ 26

1.3.1 Basic Operation ······ 26

1.3.2 Comprehensive Quality Test ······ 28

1.3.3 Competition for CEO …… 29
1.3.4 Recruitment …… 29
1.3.5 Employee Onboarding …… 29

Chapter Two Setting up a Company …… 33

Task One：Understanding Basic Company Information …… 34
2.1.1 Understanding Yourself …… 35
2.1.2 Recalling the Knowledge …… 36
2.1.3 Challenging the Memory …… 37
2.1.4 Course Characteristic …… 37

Task Two：Building the Team …… 40
2.2.1 Running for CEO …… 41
2.2.2 Organizing Team Members …… 43
2.2.3 Working with Virtual Company in ARE …… 47
2.2.4 Sending the Function Cards …… 48

Chapter Three Augmented Reality Education …… 53

Task One：Familiar with ARE …… 54
3.1.1 Special Function Cards …… 55
3.1.2 Position Cognitive Cards …… 55
3.1.3 Enterprise Cognitive Cards …… 57
3.1.4 Production Operation Cards …… 58

Task Two：Understanding Enterprise …… 66
3.2.1 Understanding the Background of Enterprise …… 67
3.2.2 Understanding the Layout of Enterprise …… 67
3.2.3 Understanding the Structure of Organization …… 68

3.2.4 Understanding the Rules of Operation ······ 68
3.2.5 Understanding the Rules of Production Capacity ······ 70
3.2.6 Understanding the Basic Situation of Operation ······ 71

Task Three: Understanding Basic Business ······ 76
3.3.1 Understanding Business System ······ 77
3.3.2 Understanding Enterprise Business Flow ······ 77
3.3.3 Understanding Raw Materials ······ 79
3.3.4 Understanding Enterprise Logistics Process ······ 80
3.3.5 Understanding Enterprise Information Flow ······ 81
3.3.6 Understanding Enterprise Capital Flow ······ 82

Task Four: Understanding Basic Position Information ······ 85
3.4.1 Understanding the Responsibility of Position ······ 86
3.4.2 Understanding the Position's Flow ······ 88
3.4.3 Understanding the Position's Report ······ 88
3.4.4 Understanding Position Sheets ······ 89
3.4.5 Understanding Position Data ······ 89

Chapter Four Business Cognition ······ 95

Task One: Collaboration of Production and Sales ······ 96
4.1.1 Understanding the Collaboration of Production and Sales ······ 97
4.1.2 Real Situation Matching with Business Receipts ······ 97
4.1.3 Practicing Collaboration of Production and Sales ······ 98
4.1.4 Summarizing the Value of Collaboration of Production and Sales ··· 98
4.1.5 Preliminary Understanding of Basic Chinese Receipts (Sample Only) ··· 99

Task Two: Collaborative Purchasing ······ 110
4.2.1 Understanding Collaborative Purchasing ······ 111

4.2.2 Real Situation Matching with Business Receipts …………………… 111
4.2.3 Practicing Collaborative Purchasing …………………………………… 112
4.2.4 Preliminary Understanding of Basic Chinese Purchasing Receipt（Sample Only）……………………………………………………………… 113

Chapter Five Evaluation …………………………………………………………… 121

Task One：General Manager Meeting ………………………………………… 122
5.1.1 Checking the Schedule of Meeting …………………………………… 123
5.1.2 General Manager Report …………………………………………………… 123
5.1.3 Meeting Content ……………………………………………………………… 124

Task Two：Analytical Thinking ……………………………………………………… 125
5.2.1 Sales Management …………………………………………………………… 126
5.2.2 Purchasing Management …………………………………………………… 126
5.2.3 Warehousing Management ………………………………………………… 127
5.2.4 Production Management …………………………………………………… 128
5.2.5 Financial Management ……………………………………………………… 128

Task Three：Evaluation ………………………………………………………………… 130
5.3.1 Evaluating Yourself ………………………………………………………… 131
5.3.2 Evaluating Each Other ……………………………………………………… 132
5.3.3 General Manager Evaluation ……………………………………………… 132
5.3.4 Composite Results …………………………………………………………… 133

Appendix 1 Initial Data in April …………………………………………………… 140

Appendix 2 Tables of Accounting Terms in Chinese and English … 144

References ……………………………………………………………………………… 168

Chapter One

Course Description

Section One: Course Background

1.1.1 Virtual Business Social Environment (VBSE)

Virtual Business Social Environment is a comprehensive practice teaching platform for colleges and universities. Through system simulation of real business social environment in typical units, departments, and positions, students can experience pre-job training in order to fully understand the modern business society. The purpose of using VBSE is to cultivate practical and technical talents.

The trained students should be able to fill in the corresponding documents and forms related to the completion of the business processes according to the requirements of the business position, and be familiar with the logical relationship between the daily work requirements of the position and the standard forms. Also, they can understand the relationship between upstream and downstream departments and the possible impact on other businesses.

VBSE's concept includes three main points. They are increasing teaching ability, enhancing enterprise business awareness and understanding position's responsibility and business processes. Experiencing business thinking and business training methods can not only help students to understand the employment demand of enterprise, but also make suggestions for business optimization.

VBSE provides the guidance system and related teaching environment for the simulation training of enterprise operation simulation internships, so students can try business decision-making of different positions and understand the relationship between job performance and organizational performance by completing corresponding job tasks in the independent selection of jobs; gain real feelings in the process of integration among three flows of enterprise (logistics flow, information flow, and capital flow); have comprehensive understandings of business management activities and major business processes; experience the business relationship among the functional departments of the enterprise, the relevant peripheral economic organizations, and management departments such as government-enterprise cooperation. Students repeatedly practice, form the intellectual activities and professional behaviors requested in real economic activities and get a understanding of enterprise job requirements.

Through different role training activities, students are engaged in economic management and improve their comprehensive implementation ability, comprehensive decision-making ability and innovative or entrepreneurial ability.

Enterprise is the basic unit of social economy, and its development is restricted by its own conditions and external environment. The competition between enterprises should not only comply with the administrative regulations of the state, but also abide by various agreements in the industry. Before starting the enterprise simulation competition, everyone should understand and be familiar with these rules in order to survive, develop, and achieve goals in competitions.

1.1.2 Augmented Reality Education (ARE)

Augmented Reality Education is an integrated and practical teaching solution based on a new scene teaching model. It relies on virtual reality, augmented reality, human-computer interaction, and other technologies and sensing equipment. With the mainstream industries and emerging industries, it constructs the virtual environment and practical teaching content. Through immersive situation, multi-dimensional audio-visual and hands-on interaction of learning, it creates a multi-sensory environment across time and space.

Augmented Reality Education platform supports multi-theme context systems, such as manufacturing industry, logistics industry, tourism industry, and e-commerce industry. In the manufacturing industry context system, teachers can lead students to immerse themselves in the manufacturing enterprise context. Through real business teaching cases, it is possible to reduce enterprise business processes, such as production, supply, marketing, storage, finance, and other work content. Using virtual reality and augmented reality technology, we can analyze information flow, capital flow, logistics flow, business flow, and document flow between the real world and the virtual world.

In the course, teachers and students enter the enterprise with a strong sense of reality and a three-dimensional sense to gain an immersive experience. At the same time, the equipment and the environment produce corresponding feedback to the participants so as to achieve deep integration and interaction between people and the environment, people and machines, and roles and positions. This learning experience is more likely to stimulate students' learning motivation, enrich their learning experiences, promote their active learning, and improve their knowledge transfer.

Section Two: Manufacturing Business Process

1.2.1 Warehousing Process

1.2.1.1 Warehousing

At the beginning of the hand-over, the manufacturing enterprise has a general warehouse for storage of finished products, semi-finished products, and raw materials.

The warehouse information is as follows:

Warehouse type	No.	Stock materials
General warehouse	N/A	Steel tube, cushion, hood, wheel, chip, economical set, comfort set, luxury set, galvanized tube, memory space cotton cushion
		Economical baby stroller's frame, comfort baby stroller's frame, luxury baby stroller's frame
		Economical baby stroller, comfort baby stroller, luxury baby stroller

The warehouse capacity information is as follows:

Warehouse type	Service life (year)	Storage area (m^2)	Warehouse volume (m^3)	Total number of storage units	Selling price (ten thousand yuan)
General warehouse	20	500	3,000	300,000	540

The stock material information is as follows:

No.	Name of stock material	Quantity of occupied storage units
P0001	Economical baby stroller	10
P0002	Comfort baby stroller	10
P0003	Luxury baby stroller	10
M0001	Economical baby stroller's frame	10
M0002	Comfort baby stroller's frame	10
M0003	Luxury baby stroller's frame	10
B0001	Steel tube	2
B0002	Galvanized tube	2
B0003	Cushion	4
B0004	Memory space cotton cushion	4
B0005	Hood	2
B0006	Wheel	1
B0008	Chip	1
B0007	Economical baby stroller's packaging set	2
B0009	Comfort baby stroller's packaging set	2
B0010	Luxury baby stroller's packaging set	2

1.2.1.2 Raw Materials and Finished Products

The Warehouse Department is responsible for storage of raw materials and finished products, including raw materials purchasing and in-warehouse, production picking ex-warehouse, production completion in-warehouse, and finished products ex-warehouse.

In manufacturing industry, raw materials are only used for production, and cannot be sold; semi-finished products are only used to complete warehousing and production picking work, and cannot be sold; finished products are only used to complete warehousing and sales work, and cannot be purchased.

The raw material information is as follows:

Name of raw material	No.	Unit	Specification	Source
Steel tube	B0001	Piece	ΦEX16/ΦIN11/L5000（mm）	Outsourcing
Galvanized tube	B0002	Piece	ΦEX16/ΦIN11/L5000（mm）	Outsourcing
Cushion	B0003	Piece	HJM500	Outsourcing
Memory space cotton cushion	B0004	Piece	HJM600	Outsourcing
Hood	B0005	Piece	HJ72*32*40	Outsourcing
Wheel	B0006	Piece	HJΦEX125/ΦIN60（mm）	Outsourcing
Chip	B0008	Piece	MCX3154A	Outsourcing
Economical baby stroller's packaging set	B0007	Set	HJTB100	Outsourcing
Comfort baby stroller's packaging set	B0009	Set	HJTB200	Outsourcing
Luxury baby stroller's packaging set	B0010	Set	HJTB300	Outsourcing

The semi-finished product information is as follows:

Name of semi-finished product	No.	Unit	Specification	Source
Economical baby stroller's frame	M0001	Piece	N/A	Self-made
Comfort baby stroller's frame	M0002	Piece	N/A	Self-made
Luxury baby stroller's frame	M0003	Piece	N/A	Self-made

The finished product information is as follows:

Name of finished product	No.	Unit	Specification	Source
Economical baby stroller	P0001	Piece	N/A	Self-made
Comfort baby stroller	P0002	Piece	N/A	Self-made
Luxury baby stroller	P0003	Piece	N/A	Self-made

1.2.1.3 Bill of Materials (BOM)

1. Economical baby stroller

Product structure diagram of economical baby stroller is as follows:

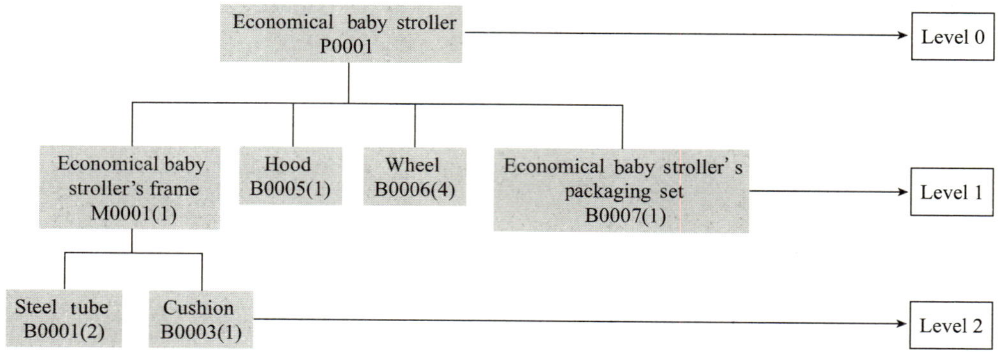

Economical baby stroller's bill of materials is as follows:

Level	Material No.	Name of material	Specification	Unit	Quantity	Notes
0	P0001	Economical baby stroller	N/A	Piece	1	Self-made finished product
1	M0001	Economical baby stroller's frame	N/A	Piece	1	Self-made semi-finished product
1	B0005	Hood	HJ72*32*40	Piece	1	Outsourcing
1	B0006	Wheel	HJΦEX125/ΦIN60（mm）	Piece	4	Outsourcing
1	B0007	Economical baby stroller's packaging set	HJTB100	Set	1	Outsourcing
2	B0001	Steel tube	ΦEX16/ΦIN11/L5000（mm）	Piece	2	Outsourcing
2	B0003	Cushion	HJM500	Piece	1	Outsourcing

2. Comfort baby stroller

Product structure diagram of comfort baby stroller is as follows:

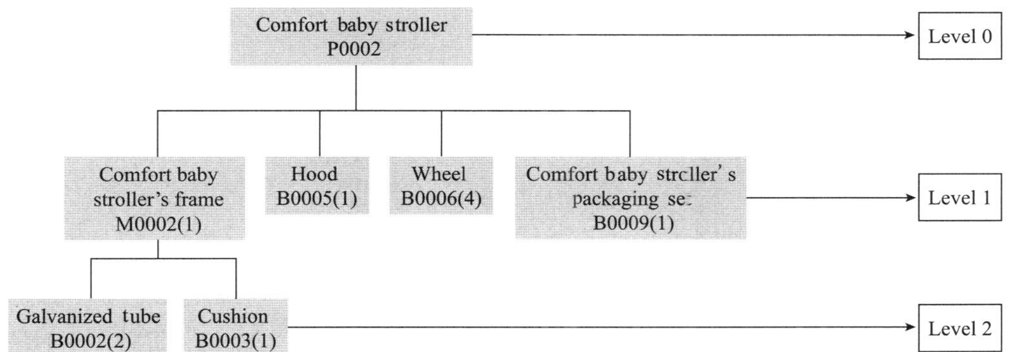

Comfort baby stroller's bill of materials is as follows:

Level	Material No.	Name of material	Specification	Unit	Quantity	Notes
0	P0002	Comfort baby stroller	N/A	Piece	1	Self-made finished product
1	M0002	Comfort baby stroller's frame	N/A	Piece	1	Self-made semi-finished product
1	B0005	Hood	HJ72*32*40	Piece	1	Outsourcing
1	B0006	Wheel	HJΦEX125/ΦIN60（mm）	Piece	4	Outsourcing
1	B0009	Comfort baby stroller's packaging set	HJTB200	Set	1	Outsourcing
2	B0002	Galvanized tube	ΦEX16/ΦIN11/L5000（mm）	Piece	2	Outsourcing
2	B0003	Cushion	HJM500	Piece	1	Outsourcing

3. Luxury baby stroller

Product structure diagram of luxury baby stroller is as follows:

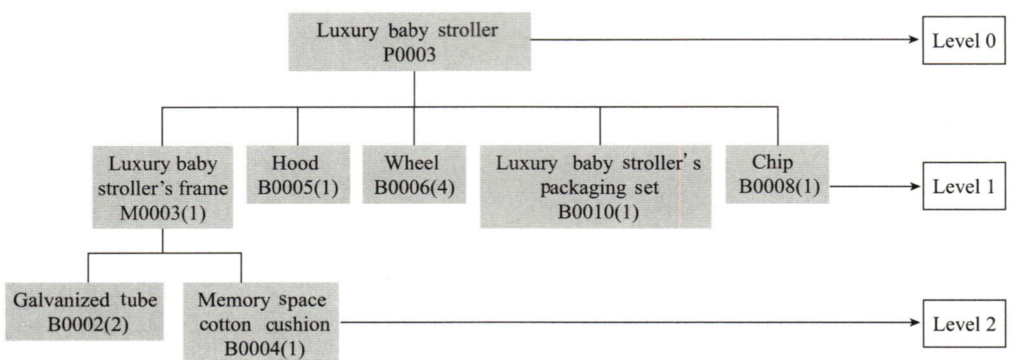

Luxury baby stroller's bill of materials is as follows:

Level	Material No.	Name of material	Specification	Unit	Quantity	Notes
0	P0003	Luxury baby stroller	N/A	Piece	1	Self-made finished product
1	M0003	Luxury baby stroller's frame	N/A	Piece	1	Self-made semi-finished product
1	B0005	Hood	HJ72*32*40	Piece	1	Outsourcing
1	B0006	Wheel	HJΦEX125/ΦIN60（mm）	Piece	4	Outsourcing
1	B0008	Chip	MCX3154A	Piece	1	Outsourcing
1	B0010	Luxury baby stroller's packaging set	HJTB300	Set	1	Outsourcing
2	B0002	Galvanized tube	ΦEX16/ΦIN 11/L5000（mm）	Piece	2	Outsourcing
2	B0004	Memory space cotton cushion	HJM600	Piece	1	Outsourcing

1.2.2 Production Process

In the virtual commercial society, manufacturing industry is the only one to be responsible for production. Enterprise production cannot be separated from the plant, production equipment, and other production sites and production facilities. At the beginning of the hand-over of manufacturing industry in VBSE, manufacturing enterprise has a large workshop with 10 general machine tools and 1 assembly line, and all equipment is undamaged and operates well.

Plant information is as follows:

Plant type	Value (ten thousand yuan)	Service life (year)	Capacity
Big plant	720	20	20 machine tools
Small plant	480	12	12 machine tools

(1) During the operation, the big plant purchased at the beginning of the hand-over shall not be sold.

(2) During the operation, if the capacity of the plant is insufficient, the manufacturing enterprise will purchase plants from the service company, while the service company only provides small plants.

(3) The relationship between plant capacity and installed equipment quantity is as follows:

① A general machine tool can be installed in a machine tool position;

② A digital machine tool can be installed in two machine tool positions;

③ An assembly line can be installed in four machine tool positions.

(4) The plant is only allowed to be sold and not allowed to be rent.

1.2.3 Equipment Rules

The equipment information is as follows:

Equipment name	Acquisition cost (ten thousand yuan)	Service life (year)	Depreciation cost (yuan/month)	Maintenance cost (yuan/month)	Production capacity			Selling price
					Economical	Comfort	Luxury	
General machine tool	21	10			500	500	N/A	Sold at book value
Digital machine tool	72	10			3,000	3,000	3,000	
Assembly line	51	10			7,000	7,000	6,000	

(1) According to the operation condition, the enterprise may purchase production equipment from the service company at any time.

(2) Depreciation: The production equipment shall be depreciated on a monthly basis. At the same time, according to the enterprise income tax law, train, ship, machinery and other production equipment shall be depreciated during a period of 10 years, excluding depreciation in the current month of purchase.

Requirements of production equipment for production workers are as follows:

Equipment name	Personnel level	Staffing requirement
General machine tool	Primary	2
Digital machine tool	Advanced	2
Assembly line	Primary	5
	Intermediate	15

The capacity of production equipment for all kinds of baby strollers is as follows:

Equipment name	Product name	Rated capacity	Department
General machine tool	Economical baby stroller's frame	10*500	Production Planning Department
	Comfort baby stroller's frame	10*500	
Digital machine tool	Economical baby stroller's frame	1*3,000	
	Comfort baby stroller's frame	1*3,000	
	Luxury baby stroller's frame	1*3,000	
Assembly line	Economical baby stroller	1*7,000	
	Comfort baby stroller	1*7,000	
	Luxury baby stroller	1*6,000	

1.2.4 Capacity Rules

According to production capacity, production equipment will be assigned to work, including dispatch, dispatch hours, and dispatch quantity. Meanwhile, the production capacity should be less than or equal to (≤) the required production capacity.

During the dispatch, one kind of products can only be produced in one specific production line. For example, if an assembly line is to arrange the production of 5,000 economical baby strollers, the remaining 2,000 production capacity cannot be used for the production of comfort baby strollers or luxury baby strollers. The production of different types of products must be arranged after all the resource capacities are finished.

During the dispatch, according to the product's bill of materials, it is necessary to check raw materials. If raw materials can not meet the production needs, they can not be dispatched.

1.2.5 Process Route

Process route is also known as processing route. It refers to the enterprise's self-made product's processing sequence and standard processing time in each process quota. It is a kind of plan management documents, mainly used for process scheduling and workshop cost statistics.

P0001—Economical baby stroller

No.	Department	Process description	Work center	Processing time
10	Production Planning Department–Machine shop	Economical baby stroller's frame processing	General (digital) machine tool	1 day
20	Production Planning Department–Assembly shop	Assembly of economical baby stroller	Assembly line	1 day

P0002—Comfort baby stroller

No.	Department	Process description	Work center	Processing time
10	Production Planning Department–Machine shop	Comfort baby stroller's frame processing	General (digital) machine tool	1 day
20	Production Planning Department–Assembly shop	Assembly of comfort baby stroller	Assembly line	1 day

P0003—Luxury baby stroller

No.	Department	Process description	Work center	Processing time
10	Production Planning Department–Machine shop	Luxury baby stroller's frame processing	Digital machine tool	1 day
20	Production Planning Department–Assembly shop	Assembly of luxury baby stroller	Assembly line	1 day

1.2.5.1 Expenses on Purchasing R&D Achievements

Default initial production permit is for economical baby stroller in the manufacturing enterprise. With the improvement of enterprise operation, the manufacturing enterprise needs to produce comfort or luxury baby stroller. The service company sells the corresponding production technology achievements to the manufacturing enterprise. Since the service company has completed the research and development of new products, the manufacturing enterprise can immediately start production.

License type	Price (yuan)
Comfort	1,000,000
Luxury	1,500,000

1.2.5.2 ISO Certification

Before production, the first thing for the manufacturing enterprise is to carry out ISO 9000 certification. Production Planning Department of the manufacturing enterprise needs to purchase ISO 9000 certification service from the service company. The specific cost for certification is 50,000 yuan each time.

1.2.5.3 3C Certification

Before sale, the manufacturing enterprise needs to obtain 3C certification. In addition, default initial production permit is for economical baby stroller. Production Planning Department of the manufacturing enterprise needs to purchase 3C certification service of the correlative products from the service company. The specific cost for certification is 22,000 yuan each time.

1.2.6 Procurement Process

In the Virtual Business Social Environment（VBSE）, raw materials in the manufacturing enterprise are purchased from the industrial and trade enterprises, which can not be purchased from other types of enterprises.

The raw material information is as follows:

No.	Name of inventory	Specification	Unit	Source	Market supply average unit price (yuan)	Market supply average unit price including tax (yuan)
B0001	Steel tube	ΦEX16/ΦIN11/L5000（mm）	Piece	Outsourcing	103.70	121.33
B0002	Galvanized tube	ΦEX16/ΦIN11/L5000（mm）	Piece	Outsourcing	169.97	198.86
B0003	Cushion	HJM500	Piece	Outsourcing	78.21	91.50
B0004	Memory space cotton cushion	HJM600	Piece	Outsourcing	215.85	252.54
B0005	Hood	HJ72*32*40	Piece	Outsourcing	140.77	164.70
B0006	Wheel	HJΦEX125/ΦIN60（mm）	Piece	Outsourcing	26.07	30.50
B0007	Economical baby stroller's packaging set	HJTB100	Set	Outsourcing	88.63	103.70
B0008	Chip	MCX3154A	Piece	Outsourcing	264.85	309.88
B0009	Comfort baby stroller's packaging set	HJTB200	Set	Outsourcing	187.69	219.60
B0010	Luxury baby stroller's packaging set	HJTB300	Set	Outsourcing	220.02	257.42

Notes: The VAT rate here is 17%.

The buyer (manufacturing enterprise) and the seller (industrial & trade enterprise) need to sign a written purchasing contract. The buyer carries out sales order, which is then confirmed by the seller; according to sales order the seller arranges the delivery, and the buyer accepts the goods. Both sides behave in accordance with the contract.

1.2.7 Sales Process

Baby strollers are sold to dealers or international trade enterprises by the Sale Department of the manufacturing enterprise. It can not be sold to other types of enterprises. The manufacturing enterprise has to sign contracts with dealers or international trade enterprises. In addition, the manufacturing enterprise has to put the order information into the system. The order information is the basis of delivery and settlement in the system.

The manufacturing enterprise can also participate in the bidding business of the bidding company. If winning the bid, the manufacturing enterprise can sell and deliver goods, make invoices, get receipts, and conduct other business activities.

Baby strollers are sold to virtual dealers of central China. Before sales, the manufacturing enterprise needs to complete market research, and launch the advertising.

1.2.8 Market Development Process

Before sales, the manufacturing enterprise has to carry out market research. The market specialist of the manufacturing enterprise needs to purchase market research service from the service company. The specific cost is 531,000 yuan for developing the central market.

The service company can be commissioned by the manufacturing enterprise to carry out market research in the central market. The manufacturing enterprise must develop the central market in China, so the cost of advertising increases. Meanwhile it should select the market according to the cost.

The finished product information is as follows:

No.	Name of inventory	Unit	Specification	Market supply average unit price (yuan)	Market supply average unit price including tax (yuan)
P0001	Economical baby stroller	Piece			
P0002	Comfort baby stroller	Piece			
P0003	Luxury baby stroller	Piece			

1.2.9 Financial Process

(1) There are three ways of settlement. They are cash settlement, transfer check settlement, and telegraphic transfer settlement respectively. In principle, when the amount of money is less than 2,000 yuan, cash settlement can be used; when it is more than 2,000 yuan, transfer check settlement (except travel expenses or payment to personal business) can be used in daily economic activities. Transfer check settlement is used in the same bill trade. Off-site payment generally uses telegraphic transfer settlement.

(2) Type of tax: value-added tax, enterprise income tax, personal income tax, city maintenance and construction tax and additional tax of education.

① Value-added tax: the VAT rate applicable for sales and purchase of goods is 17%.

② Enterprise income tax: 25% of the total profit.

③ Individual income tax: the threshold of individual income tax is 3,500 yuan (applicable to wage and salary income). Over 3,500 yuan, individual income tax should be paid. According to the seven-level progressive tax rate, individual income tax shall be collected and remitted by the enterprise. Individuals can not pay individual income tax on their own.

The tax rate is as follows:

Level	Taxable income for the whole month	Tax rate (%)	Quick deduction (yuan)
1	*S*<1,500 yuan	3	0
2	1,500 yuan<*S*<4,500 yuan	10	105
3	4,500 yuan<*S*<9,000 yuan	20	555
4	9,000 yuan<*S*<35,000 yuan	25	1,005
5	35,000 yuan<*S*<55,000 yuan	30	2,755
6	55,000 yuan<*S*<80,000 yuan	35	5,505
7	*S*>80,000 yuan	45	13,505

④ City maintenance and construction tax: 7% of VAT.

⑤ Additional tax of education: 3% of VAT.

(3) Inventory valuation:

① According to monthly weighted average method, material costs are included in direct material costs; inventory costs are included in direct management costs; costs of purchasing materials are included in indirect management costs.

② Monthly weighted average correlation calculation:

◈ Material average unit price= (opening inventory quantity × inventory unit price + actual purchase in-warehousing amount of this month) / (opening inventory quantity + actual in-warehousing quantity of this month);

◈ Material issue cost = quantity of material issued this month × average unit price of material.

③ Acquisition and depreciation of fixed assets:

Fixed assets are acquired by purchase. Fixed assets purchased in the current month are not depreciated, and the depreciation shall be accrued by the following month; fixed assets sold in the current month have to calculate depreciation, it shall not be accrued by the next month. Depreciation of fixed assets is accrued on a straight-line basis.

The depreciation information is as follows:

Name of fixed assets	Service life (month)	Start date	Original value (yuan)	Residual value (yuan)	Monthly depreciation amount (yuan)
Office	240	2014.9.15	12,000,000.00	600,000.00	47,500.00
General warehouse	240	2014.9.15	5,400,000.00	270,000.00	21,375.00
Big plant	240	2014.9.15	7,200,000.00	360,000.00	28,500.00
General machine tool	120	2014.9.15	210,000.00	–	1,750.00
Assembly line	120	2014.9.15	510,000.00	–	4,250.00
Computer	48	2014.9.15	6,000.00	–	125.00

(4) Collection and distribution of manufacturing costs:

① The costs incurred by the Production Management Department and the common indirect costs of each workshop in the production process are included in the manufacturing costs;

② Manufacturing costs, according to the costs of the workshop, set up a new classification item—machining workshop, and assembly workshop;

③ Machining workshop costs, such as wages of workers, machining workshop equipment depreciation and maintenance costs, will be included in manufacturing costs of machining workshop. Similarly, the costs of assembly workshop are included in manufacturing costs of assembly workshop;

④ Management costs include the wage of superintendence of the Production Planning Department, depreciation of equipment, and reimbursement of office expenses.

⑤ Plant depreciation is included in manufacturing costs. At the same time, the way of allocation is according to the proportion of plant space occupied by various types of equipment.

(5) Costing process:

① Production cost is divided into direct material cost, labor cost and manufacturing cost carried forward;

② The cost of the workshop in the manufacturing costs is directly included in the production cost of the workshop, and if the workshop has two or more products, the workshop manufacturing costs are distributed according to the production hours of the products;

③ For unfinished product, only material cost is calculated, and manufacturing cost and labor cost are not calculated.

◈ Current production cost = initial production cost (direct material) + current collection of direct labor + current collection of manufacturing cost.

(6) Cost collection process:

◈ Raw material cost = material out-warehousing issued quantity × average unit price of the material;

The labor cost is the staff salary of the Production Department in the current month, including production management personnel and production workers.

(7) Semi-finished product accounting process:

Take frame for example. Frame is part of the semi-finished product. Costs of frame (including cost of frame purchasing, labor cost of assembling and manufacturing cost) are included in production costs.

(8) Cost distribution of products:

If different products are produced in the same workshop, the direct manufacturing costs and indirect manufacturing costs carried forward in the workshop are allocated based on the completed quantities of each kind of products.

(9) Bad debt losses:

① Production and manufacturing enterprises use the allowance method to calculate the loss of bad debts;

② Provision for bad debts shall be drawn each year, by 3% of the accounts receivable at the end of the year;

③ Debts that have not been recovered for more than one year are recognized as bad debt losses. Bad debt losses of accounts receivable don't mean that the company should waive collection right. If bad debt accounts are receivable in a future period, the company has the right to recover debts.

(10) Profit distribution:

The profit distribution of the company shall be carried out in accordance with the statutory procedures. According to the stipulation of the company, the statutory surplus reserve fund shall be drawn by 10% of the net profit of the year. Any surplus reserve fund shall be drawn by the resolutions of the board of directors.

(11) Bill usage process:

① Checks are used by various enterprises. The bank charges the service fee. The user must purchase and use them at the bank. Enterprises or individuals can not make checks by themselves.

② The check is sold per sheet by the bank, and the enterprise shall include the fee in the financial expenses.

③ Enterprises make a sound bill registration system for inspection.

④ Invoices used by enterprises: VAT special invoices.

⑤ VAT input tax needs to be declared, authenticated, and paid.

⑥ In the process of purchasing goods or services, the settlement of both parties must base on the invoice, and the settlement business cannot be carried out without the invoice.

⑦ The tax bureau will check the use of invoices anytime, meanwhile, the tax bureau has the right to give an administrative fine to the company which uses nonstandard invoices.

1.2.10 Human Resources Process

The employee information is as follows:

Department	Name of position	Level of position	Quantity	Direct superior
Enterprise Management Department	General Manager	General Manager	1	Board of directors
	Administrative assistant	Functional Manager	1	General Manager

Continued

Department	Name of position	Level of position	Quantity	Direct superior
Marketing Department	Marketing Manager	Department Manager	1	General Manager
	Marketing specialist	Functional Manager	1	Department Manager
	Sales specialist	Functional Manager	1	Department Manager
Production Planning Department	Production Planning Manager	Department Manager	1	General Manager
	Workshop administrator	Functional Manager	1	Department Manager
	Production planner	Functional Manager	1	Department Manager
	Primary production worker	Worker	25	Workshop administrator
	Intermediate production worker	Worker	15	Workshop administrator
Warehousing Department	Warehouse Manager	Department Manager	1	General Manager
	Warehouse keeper	Functional Manager	1	Department Manager
Purchasing Department	Purchasing Manager	Department Manager	1	General Manager
	Buyer	Functional Manager	1	Department Manager
Human Resources Department	Human Resources Manager	Department Manager	1	General Manager
	Human resources assistant	Functional Manager	1	Department Manager
Financial Department	Financial Manager	Department Manager	1	General Manager
	Cashier	Functional Manager	1	Department Manager
	Financial accountant	Functional Manager	1	Department Manager
	Cost accountant	Functional Manager	1	Department Manager

The compensation information is as follows:

Employee type	Basic salary
General Manager	12,000 yuan/month
Department Manager	7,500 yuan/month
Functional Manager	5,500 yuan/month
Marketing staff	4,500 yuan/month
Junior / intermediate / senior production worker	3,600 yuan/month, 4,000 yuan/month, 4,600 yuan/month

(1) Compensation items:

✓ Basic wages;

✓ Pension insurance;

✓ Medical insurance;

✓ Maternity insurance;

✓ Unemployment insurance;

✓ Industrial injury insurance;

✓ Housing provident fund;

✓ Withholding personal income tax;

✓ Dismissal compensation.

① If enterprises want to dismiss employees, they need to pay three months of basic salary as dismissal compensation;

② The salary for the same month of dismissal is calculated according to the following process:

❖ The salary for the same month of dismissal = actual working days × (basic salary / full-time working days for the month) + retirement benefits.

(2) Attendance management:

✓ Monthly attendance is implemented in VBSE. Because only two virtual working days are designed per month, attendance statistics are calculated according to the following process:

◈ Employee attendance days = virtual attendance days of the current month / total virtual working days of the current month × 21.75;

◈ Employee attendance days = 21.75 − employee absence days;

◈ Attendance period: the monthly attendance period shall be from the 26th of this month to the 25th of the following month.

Five kinds of social insurance and housing provident fund contribution rate are as follows:

Type	Pension insurance	Unemployment insurance	Industrial injury insurance	Maternity insurance	Medical insurance		Housing provident fund
					Basic medical insurance	Massive mutual assistance insurance	
Company	20%	1.5%	0.5%	0.8%	9%	1%	10%
Individual	8%	0.5%	0	0	2%	3%	10%

1.2.11 Logistics Process

(1) Logistics transportation works for the purchase and sale business between industrial and trade enterprises and manufacturing enterprises, and between manufacturing enterprises and dealers.

(2) Logistics costs are usually paid by buyers;

(3) Logistics fee is 5% of the value of goods.

Section Three: System Operation Training

1.3.1 Basic Operation

1.3.1.1 Homepage

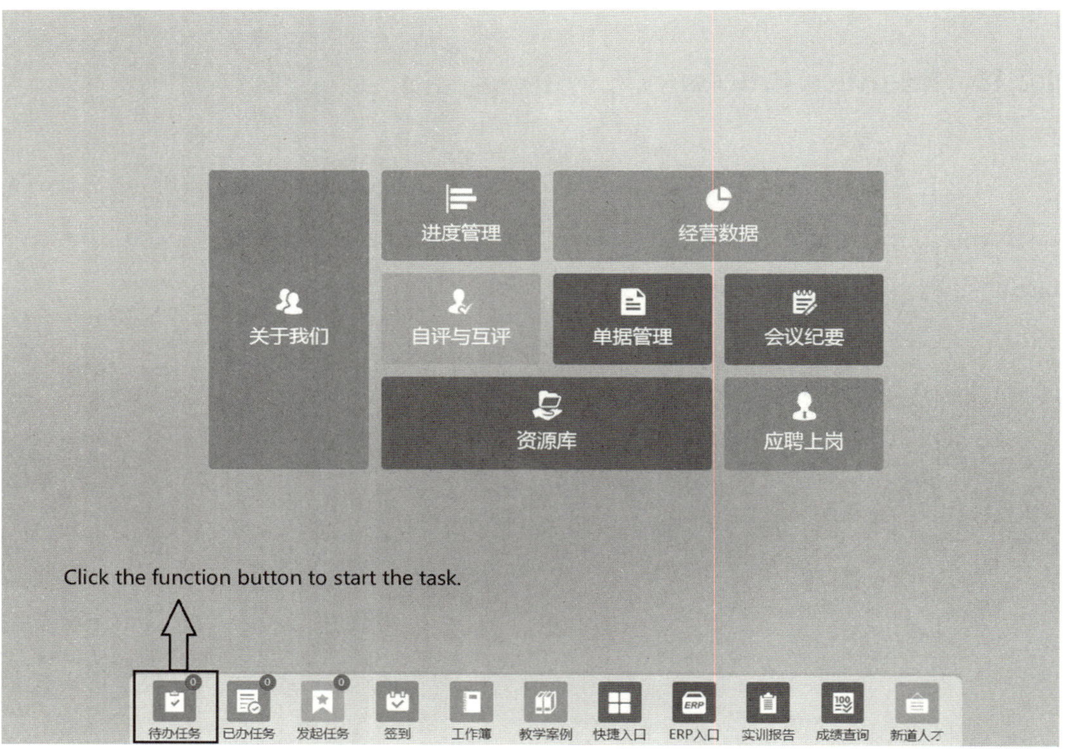

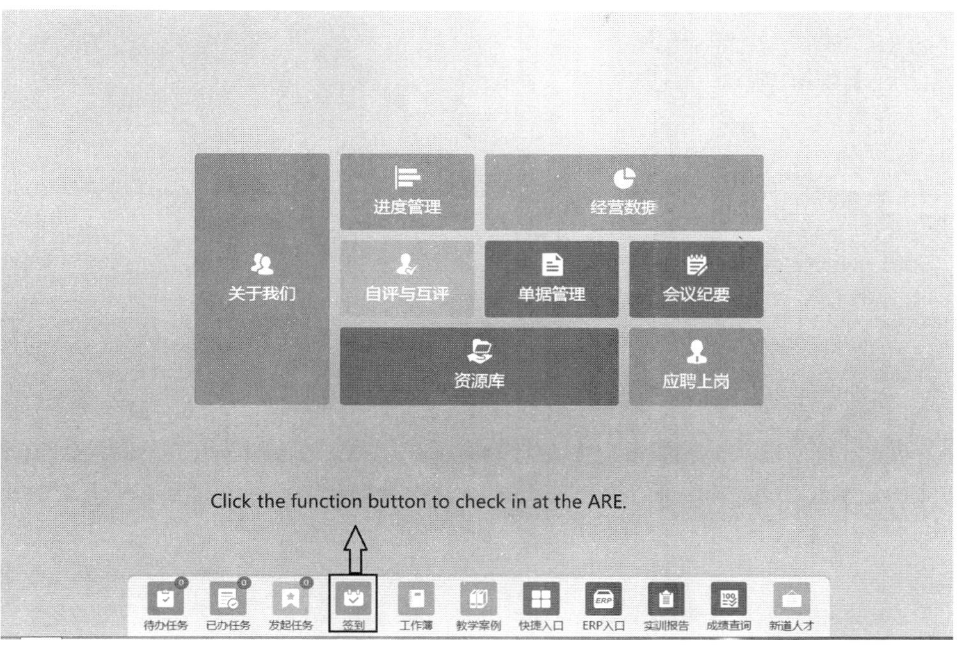

1.3.1.2 Enrolling

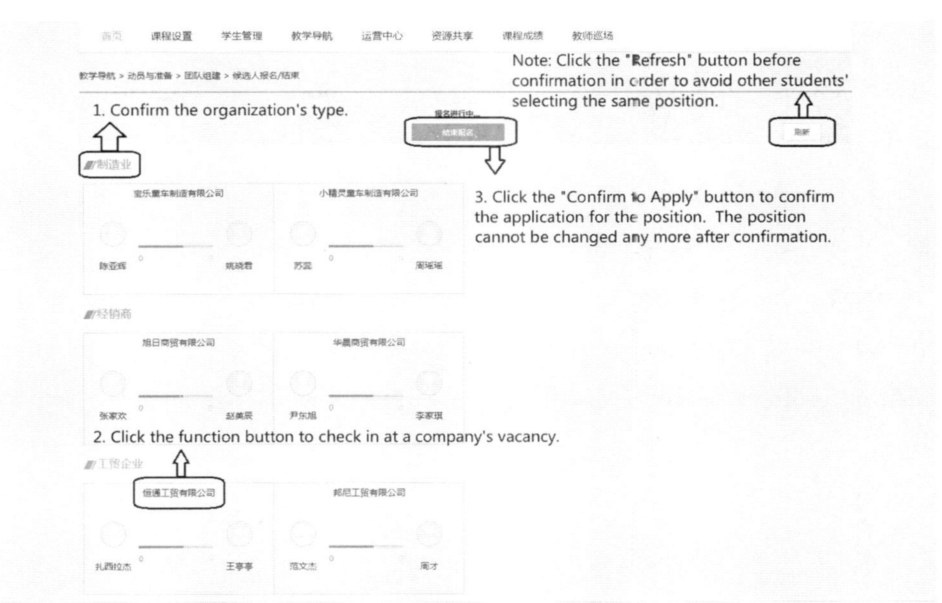

1.3.1.3 Polling

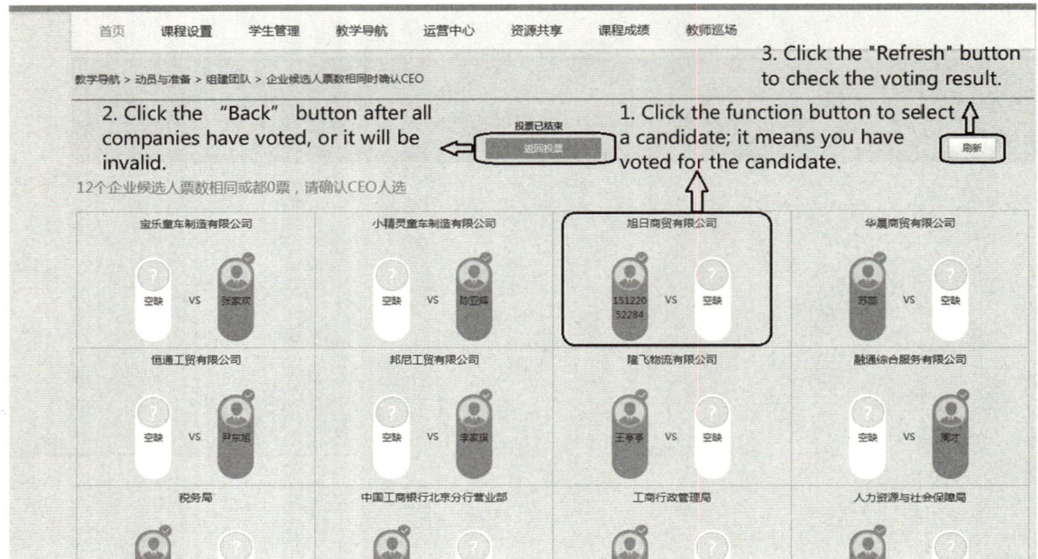

1.3.2 Comprehensive Quality Test

Before entering the internship position, we will do the comprehensive quality test for all the students. Internship system will automatically generate the topic. The topic types include basic quality, general management, marketing, purchase, production, storage, human resources, public administration and finance.

During the simulation of the internship, the system will grade automatically, the student with the highest score being the CEO candidate. Other CEO candidates are produced according to personal thoughts and teacher's recommendations.

1.3.3 Competition for CEO

CEO (Chief Executive Officer) is the senior manager in charge of daily operation and management in the enterprise. CEO is responsible to the company's board of directors, and has the right of final execution and management decisions within the company.

CEO of each team is determined by the way of election in the company's panoramic, simulative and comprehensive internship system.

✓ Presentation. Candidates present their understanding of the position, value proposition, and principles of handling.

✓ All students participating in the internship can run for election.

1.3.4 Recruitment

In order to quickly set up a company's management team, CEO needs to recruit the director of human resources immediately. Then, CEO makes the recruitment posters and job requirements, together with the director of human resources. They also have to collect résumés and conduct interviews.

Each student submits his or her résumé for different positions, and after a two-way selection, the positions will be finalized.

Each student has to give full attention to this interview and prepare for it.

1.3.5 Employee Onboarding

There are two situations about employee onboarding.

Situation 1: Onboarding of students without position. (Including the students who participated in the CEO election, but failed, and who didn't participate in the CEO election)

Situation 2: Onboarding of students with position.(CEO)

◇ Onboarding of students without position

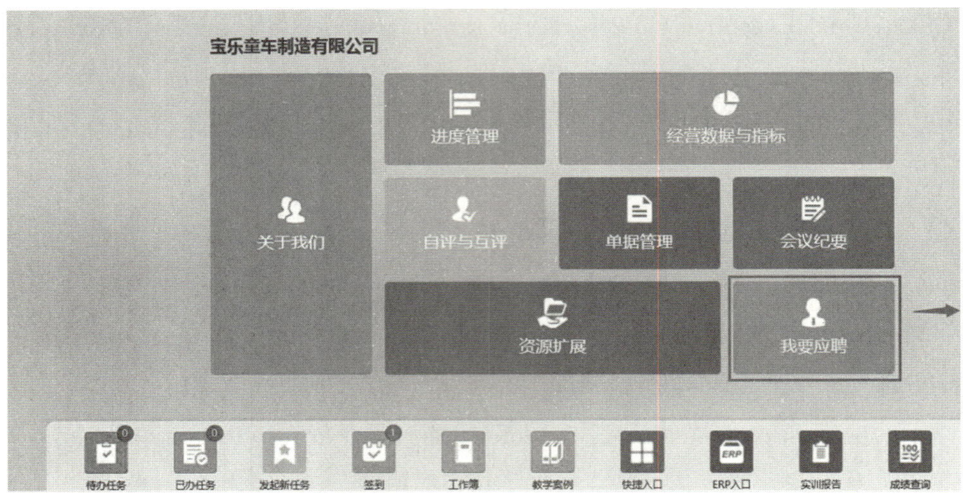

In the homepage click on the "I want to apply" button into the onboarding page.

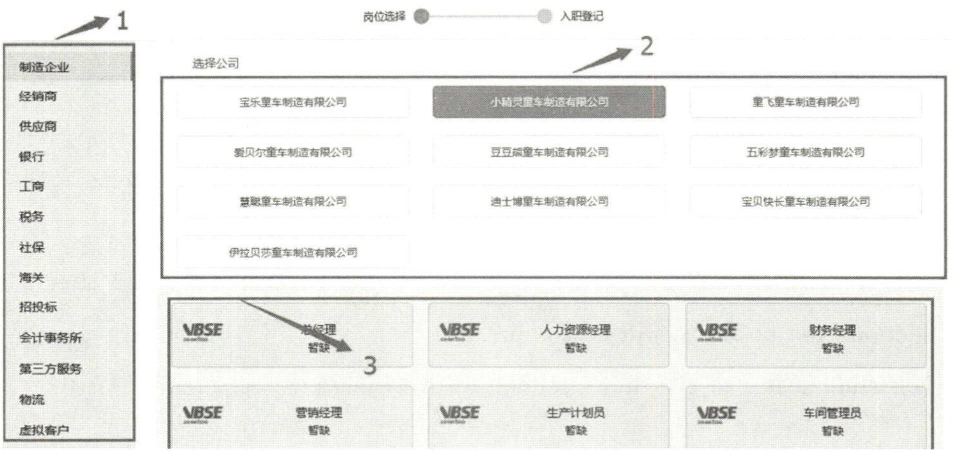

Select the organization in Zone 1;

Select the enterprise in Zone 2;

Select the position in Zone 3.

岗位选择 ——— 入职登记

入职登记表

姓名		性别		图片 点击上传
院（系）		专业		
班级		学号		
手机号码		邮箱		
身份证号				
已选择岗位				
爱好和特长				
工作经历				
自我定位				

上一步　　提交

Fill in the basic personal information, then click on "Submit".

◇ Onboarding of students with position

In the homepage click on the "I want to apply" button into the onboarding page.

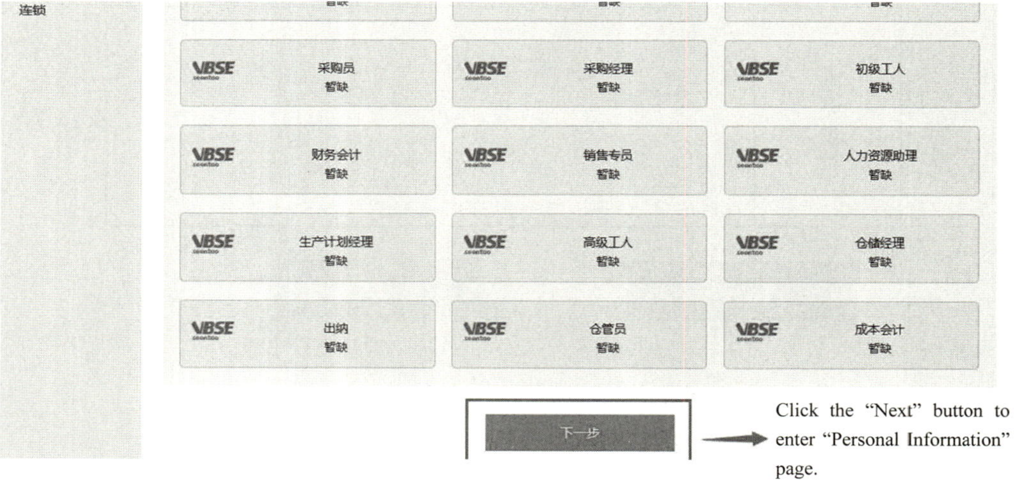

Click the "Next" button to enter "Personal Information" page.

Click on the "Next" button, and then enter the "Personal Information" page.

Chapter Two

Setting up a Company

Task One: Understanding Basic Company Information

Main Content

1. Recalling the knowledge
2. Challenging the memory
3. Course characteristic
4. Test of right hemisphere

Knowledge Points

1. Basic company information
2. Course map
3. Five steps of teaching platform

◇ Target of the task

1. Learning basic company information
2. Learning the main target of five steps of teaching platform
3. Training the memory

2.1.1 Understanding Yourself

✓ According to the questionnaire, finish the questions as soon as possible.

According to your feeling, finish the questions in the questionnaire. (5=Satisfactory, 4=Relatively satisfactory, 3=Acceptable, 2=Dissatisfactory, 1=Quite dissatisfactory)												
No.	Program	Content	Before the lessons					After the lessons				
			5	4	3	2	1	5	4	3	2	1
1	Structure of enterprise	Can you image the overall structure of enterprise?										
2	Business processes	Can you fully understand the logistics flow, capital flow and information flow in the enterprise?										
3	Knowledge perception	Can you build a team with 4-6 team members, and organize them well?										
4	Position understanding	Can you fully understand the responsibility of the position ?										
5	Management planning	Can you fully understand the importance of making schedule?										
6	Receipts and reports	Can you fully understand the meaning of receipts and reports?										
7	Cooperative capability	Can you fully understand the importance of the cooperation between different departments?										
8	Communication capability	Do you know how important it is to communicate with other departments?										
9	Operation	In the management process, can you find the problems of operation?										

Continued

According to your feeling, finish the questions in the questionnaire. (5=Satisfactory, 4=Relatively satisfactory, 3=Acceptable, 2=Dissatisfactory, 1=Quite dissatisfactory)												
No.	Program	Content	Before the lessons					After the lessons				
			5	4	3	2	1	5	4	3	2	1
10	Logic	If you were the boss, could you take into consideration all of the business processes such as employment, capital, supplier and sales?										

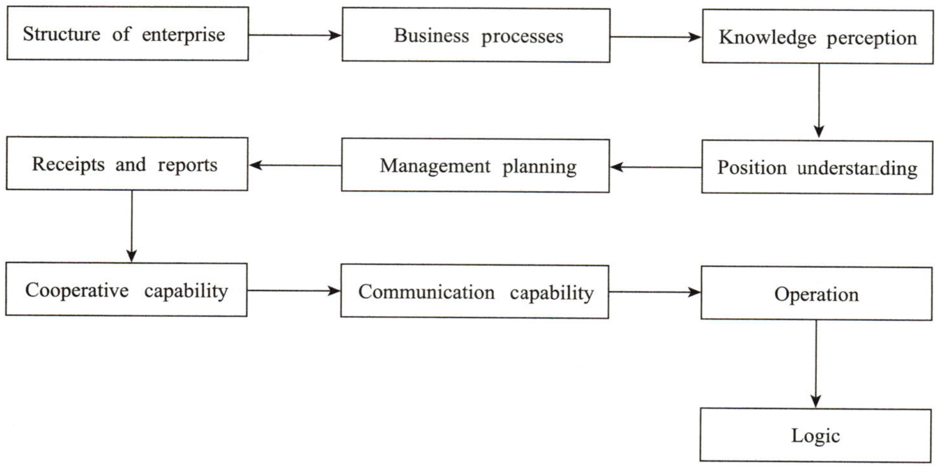

2.1.2 Recalling the Knowledge

✓ Please write the key words you think of quickly according to the topic.

◇ [I would like to say] If I become a manager in a department or manage an enterprise when I graduate, what kind of knowledge or skills can I not hold?

◇ [I would like to say] If I become a manager in a department or manage an enterprise when I graduate, what kind of knowledge or skills can I hold well?

2.1.3 Challenging the Memory

Recalling the memory	Text version	Image version
Where is your classroom?		
Where is your seat in the classroom?		
When you leave the classroom, which path do you need to pass?		
Before you turn right into the outside classroom, what do you see?		
When you go downstairs, what do you see?		

2.1.4 Course Characteristic

✓ Please match the pictures with texts.

A

B

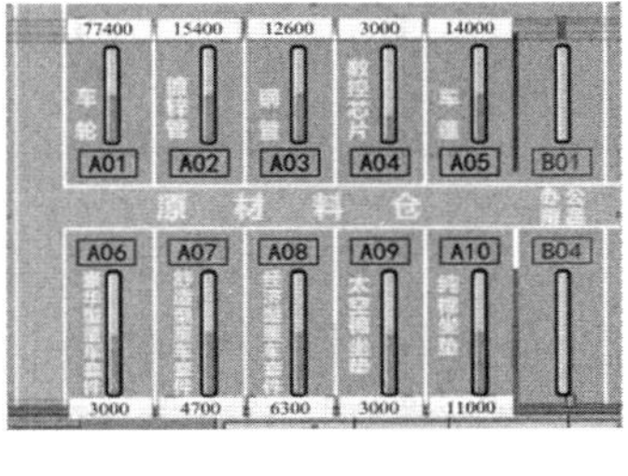

C

A. The e-board of raw material

B. Service interworking

C. Display the data of raw material cabin

(　　) 1. Combine with business and real situaticn. ARE designs a lot of real situations which make business-related concepts, receipts and flow diagram for students to fully understand business process.

(　　) 2. Combine with concepts and images. According to the research, ARE finds a new way to cultivate students' long-term memory, which puts concepts and images together. In ARE, we use this theory to help students learn more business concepts.

(　　) 3. Combine with global view and details. According to the cognitive psychology theory, students will fully understand the basic business processes through the training of logic, language, perception, and memory. In addition, ARE can combine with enterprise's details and enterprise's vision and mission.

Subtask One: Test of right hemisphere.

✓ Please use your instinct to finish the text.

1. For the makeup and hair style, you will (　　).

A. always want to change

B. sometimes want to change

C. never want to change

2. If you have to make a decision immediately, you will (　　).

A. listen to your instinct

B. do it quickly for small things and earnestly for big things

C. feel it is hard to make a decision

3. As to making a plan of trip, you will (　　).

A. be willing to adventure

B. normally not adventure, but you are willing to change the plan sometimes because of other suggestions

C. make a decision very carefully

4. When reading the biographical literature, you will (　　).

A. think if that is true

B. mostly accept the content, but sometimes will doubt

C. never doubt its content

5. Your friend tells you that you have to pay more attention to another friend, you will (　　).

A. contact first, and then make judgment

B. treat her/him carefully

C. look normal, but keep a sharp lookout for her/him silently

6. When reading an instruction book, you will ( ).

A. only see some necessary details

B. read it from start to end

C. read it from start to end carefully

7. When watching a movie, you will ( ).

A. sit on the right side B. sit on the left side

8. As to school subjects, you are good at ( ).

A. geometry B. algebra

9. As to the exhibition, you will ( ).

A. watch it according to your hobby B. watch it in sequence

10. When you are busy with what you love to do, will you forget the work? ( ).

A. Yes B. No

Results:

1–6, A = 5 points, B = 3 points, C = 1 point; 7–10, A = 3 points, B = 1 point

◈ Above or equal to 30 points: The right type. Congratulations! Nowadays, more and more people are of the right type, who like to try new things and are full of imagination.

◈ Below or equal to 29 points: The left type. Now, you have to train your RIGHT hemisphere!

Task Two: Building the Team

Main Content

1. How to run for CEO
2. How to organize team members
3. How to challenge the position
4. How to use the function cards

Knowledge Points

1. The meaning of building the team
2. The meaning of team members

◇ Target of the task

1. Learning the meaning of building the team
2. Learning the meaning of team members
3. Training the ability of organization

2.2.1 Running for CEO

✓ Please think about if you would like to run for CEO rather than other normal positions.

I would like to run for CEO	I would not like to run for CEO
Advantages: 1. 2. 3.	I am interested in ( ) position, and my reasons are: 1. 2. 3.
If I were CEO, I would promise: 1. 2. 3.	If I were ( ), I would promise: 1. 2. 3.

Subtask Two: Comprehensive ability test.

✓ According to the questions, fully understand your entrepreneurial ability. There are eight parts:

A. Innovation ability;

B. Analysis ability;

C. Predictive ability;

D. Strain ability;

E. Organizational and coordination ability;

F. Social ability;

G. Inspiring ability;

H. Learning ability.

Tests:

1. Your idea always makes other people surprise. (Y/N)

2. In general, you always think about the questior in your own way instead of learning from others. (Y/N)

3. You are always attracted by an innovative idea or a new product advertisement. (Y/N)

4. When you deal with a problem, you will prepare more than two solutions, then choose the one which you think best. (Y/N)

5. You do not like keeping on the rails. (Y/N)

6. When you plan a trip, you will plan any details. (Y/N)

7. You fully understand your advantages and disadvantages, and you know how to use your advantages and avoid your disadvantages. (Y/N)

8. You will calm down in case of emergency. (Y/N)

9. If you think this clothes is very nice, even though other people do not think so, you will still wear this clothes. (Y/N)

10. When you are in trouble, if there is a bad way to solute, you will use that way. (Y/N)

11. In the whole situation, you can finger out the details other people cannot find out. (Y/N)

12. You make an appointment with your customer, then too late to go back home, so you look for a hotel and book a room immediately. (Y/N)

13. You fully understand your balance. (Y/N)

14. You have your own opinions about your best friend's career planning in the next five years. (Y/N)

15. According to the policy, you can judge the economic trend in the next five years. (Y/N)

16. You will ask other people for help in case of emergency. (Y/N)

17. You are interested in news, and you would like to spend time in researching the background information. (Y/N)

18. You would like to talk with your colleagues and know how the company operates. (Y/N)

19. You read book all the time. (Y/N)

20. You think the performance and reward mechanism should be combined. (Y/N)

21. As the team leader, if your team member makes a mistake, you will communicate with him/her privately. (Y/N)

22. Focus on the employees' hobbies. (Y/N)

23. You always like to communicate with your friends and colleagues. (Y/N)

Results:

(1–23, Y=1 point, N =0 point)

Scores≥18 points, it means you have excellent entrepreneurial thinking;

9 points ≤ scores <18 points, it means you have good entrepreneurial thinking;

Scores<9 points, it means you have to think which part you would like to improve in entrepreneurial ability.

2.2.2 Organizing Team Members

✓ According to the résumé, we can select our team members.

Résumé
PERSONAL Name: Gender: Age: Health: Hobbies: Personality:
OBJECTIVE ① ② ③
EDUCATION ① ②

Continued

<table>
<tr><td>③

④</td></tr>
<tr><td><u>WORKING EXPERIENCE</u>

①

◈ TIME:

◈ POSITION:

◈ EXPERIENCE:

②

◈ TIME:

◈ POSITION:

◈ EXPERIENCE:</td></tr>
<tr><td><u>KNOWLEDGE BACKGROUND</u>

Hardware

Software

Language

Specialty</td></tr>
<tr><td><u>VOLUNTEER</u>

①

②</td></tr>
<tr><td><u>CONTACT</u>

✓ Address:

✓ Phone:

✓ Cell Phone:

✓ Email:</td></tr>
</table>

Then, according to different résumés we choose three same characteristics:

1.

2.

3.

Think about the characteristics of each member, we decide:

General Manager—

Manager of Sales Department—

Manager of Production Department—

Manager of Storage Department—

Manager of Procurement Department—

Manager of Financial Department—

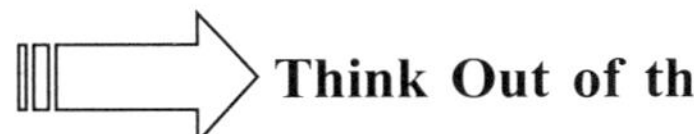

Think Out of the Box

Table 1: Assessing Which Company Departments Are Customer-minded

R&D
1. They spend time meeting customers and listening to their problems.
2. They welcome the involvement of marketing, manufacturing, and other departments in each new project.
3. They benchmark competitors' products and seek "best of class" solutions.
4. They solicit customer reactions and suggestions as the project progresses.
5. They continuously improve and refine the product on the basis of market feedback.
Purchasing
1. They proactively search for the best suppliers.
2. They build long-term relationships with fewer but more reliable, high-quality suppliers.
3. They do not compromise quality for price saving.
Manufacturing
1. They invite customers to visit and tour their plants.
2. They visit customer plants.
3. They willingly work overtime to meet promised delivery schedules.
4. They continuously search for ways to produce goods faster and/or at lower cost.
5. They continuously improve product quality, aiming for zero defect.
6. They meet customer requirements for "customization" where possible.

Continued

Marketing 1. They study customer needs and wants in well-defined market segments. 2. They allocate marketing effort in relation to the long-run profit potential of the targeted segments. 3. They develop competitive offers for each target segment. 4. They measure company image and customer satisfaction on a continuous basis. 5. They continuously gather and evaluate ideas for new products, product improvements, and services. 6. They urge all company departments and employees to be customer-centered.
Sales 1. They have specialized knowledge of the customer's industry. 2. They strive to give the customer "the best solution". 3. They make only promises that they can keep. 4. They give feedback on customers' needs and ideas to those in charge of product development. 5. They serve the same customers for a long period of time.
Logistics 1. They set a high standard for service delivery time and meet this standard consistently. 2. They operate a knowledgeable and friendly customer service department that can answer questions, handle complaints, and resolve problems in a satisfactory and timely manner.
Accounting 1. They prepare periodic "profitability" reports on products, market segments, geographic areas (regions, sales territories), order sizes, channels, and individual customers. 2. They prepare invoices tailored to customer needs and answer customer queries courteously and quickly.
Finance 1. They understand and support marketing expenditures (e.g. image advertising) that produce long-term customer preference and loyalty. 2. They tailor the financial package to the customer's financial requirements. 3. They make quick decisions on customer creditworthiness.
Public Relations 1. They send out favorable news about the company and "strictly control" unfavorable news. 2. They act as an internal customer and publicly advocate for better company policies and practices.

2.2.3 Working with Virtual Company in ARE

✓ We will follow three steps to check the information of the position in order to preliminarily understand enterprise.

Step 1 Choose the business pattern (using the login card to rotate the half circle).

Step 2 Choose the class (using the login card to rotate the half circle).

Step 3 Use the login card to draw the password.

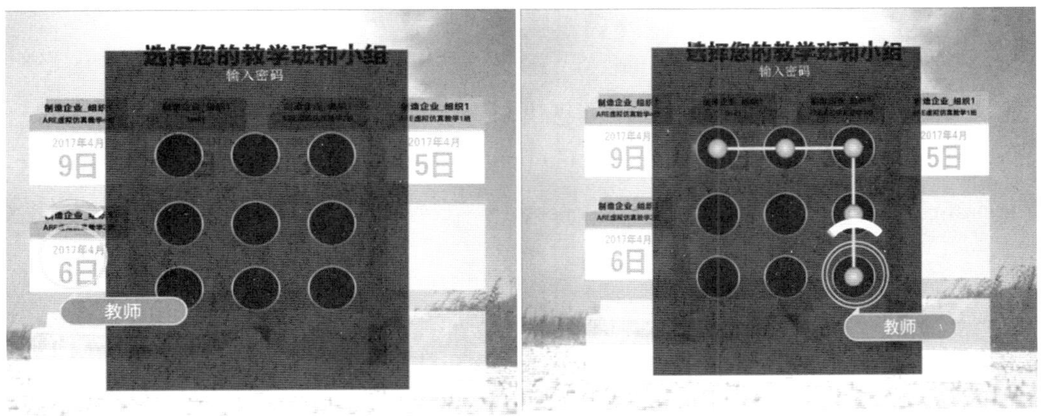

✓ Please plan the positions of CEO, Sales Manager, Financial Manager, Production Manager, Storage Manager and Purchasing Manager.

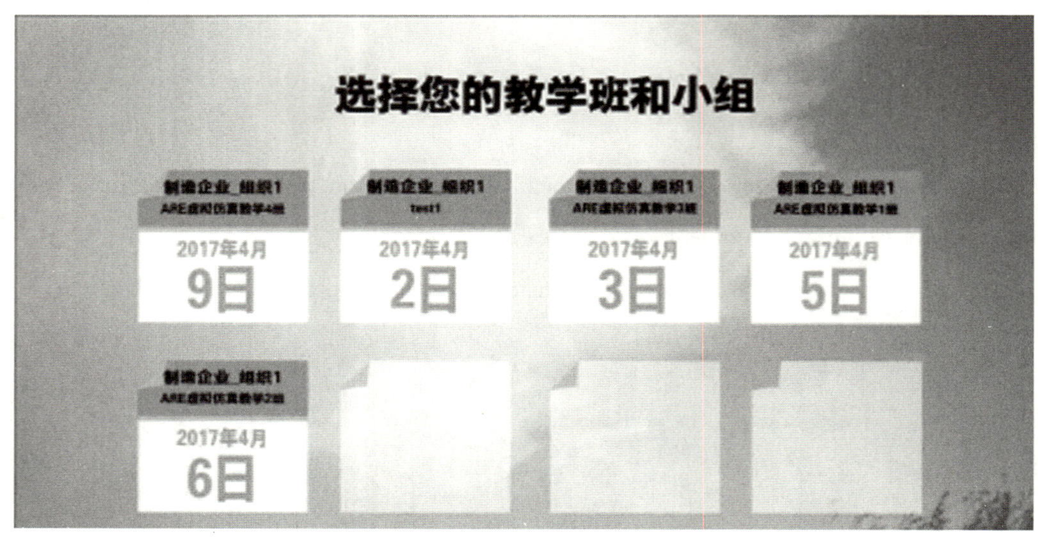

2.2.4 Sending the Function Cards

Positions		The Function Cards
CEO (4 cards)	—	Login card, enterprise visiting card, enterprise introduction card, and CEO card
Sales Manager (2 cards)	—	Production and marketing card, Sales Manager card
Purchasing Manager (2 cards)	—	Cooperative purchasing card, Purchasing Manager card
Production Manager (3 cards)	—	Manufacturing execution card, BOM card, Production Manager card
Storage Manager (9 cards)	—	Drawing material cards (3), finishing warehousing cards (3), Storage Manager cards (3)
Financial Manager (2 cards)	—	Database card, Financial Manager card

Think Out of the Box

The Criteria of Selecting the Project

1. Grasp the timing of the project and examine the absence of the project;
2. Do market segment, and further select the project with advantageous resources;
3. Strengthen the team's leadership and ability to quickly invest in the market.

According to the theory, write your thoughts:

The Seven Steps of Selecting the Good Project

Step 1 Analyze if the project is familiar to you;

Step 2 Analyze if the project is operating in local market;

Step 3 Evaluate the project's sustainable management;

Step 4 Evaluate the financial strength;

Step 5 Field trip;

Step 6 Evaluate the risk;

Step 7 Select the suitable project.

According to the seven steps, write your opinions:

Expansion of Mind

Table 2: Projects Suitable for College Students to Run

Project type	Main points
Specialty catering	1. Correct site selection 2. Actual creative selling points 3. Stable customer group 4. Food hygiene
Clothing & shoes shop	1. Correct site selection 2. Shop decoration 3. Brand selection 4. Fully understand wholesale clothing market all over the country

Continued

Project type	Main points
Hairdressing & fitness	1. Correct site selection 2. Fully understand the industry's skills and experience 3. Focus on female customers 4. Pay more attention to product feature
Health care	1. Understand the industry's limits and requirements 2. Have a certain amount of capital 3. Guidance from the industry veterans 4. Underfunded entrepreneurs can choose service industry
Liquidation	1. Choose companies with good equipment and technique 2. Pay more attention to fast service 3. Choose large and medium-size cities 4. Big investment and slow return on capital
Agricultural cultivation	1. Beware of fraud 2. Need planting experience 3. Study in a professional base
Car care	1. Good market outlook 2. Low cost and high profit 3. Need professional talents
Fashion home furnishing	1. Product positioning accuracy 2. Clear consumer groups 3. There are many channels
Gift toys	1. Correct site selection 2. Owner's taste 3. Pay more attention to handmade articles
Education training	1. Infants and children education and small language training market is wide 2. Owners are well-educated 3. Initial investment is not too much 4. Famous teachers can expand influence

Continued

Project type	Main points
E-commence	1. Fully understand internet model 2. Be good at promotion on internet 3. Could join in internet trading platform
High-tech	1. Need professional talents 2. Need professional technology 3. Capital investment

Chapter Three

Augmented Reality Education

Task One: Familiar with ARE

Main Content

1. How to use the function cards
2. How to use the position cards
3. How to use the enterprise cards
4. How to use the production and operation cards

Knowledge Points

1. The meaning of the special function cards
2. The meaning of the platform

◇ Target of the task

1. Learning the meaning of the special function cards
2. Learning the meaning of the platform

3.1.1 Special Function Cards

√ Please read the related information about special function cards and then answer the following questions.

1. [Multiple choices] Which are the right ways for login cards ? ( )

A. Using login cards when transferring from teaching video to teaching model.

B. Using login cards when transferring among different classes.

C. Using login cards when quitting interface.

D. Using login cards when transferring from Sales Manager cards to other position cards.

E. Using login cards for production.

F. The way of using login cards is rotating the half circle.

3.1.2 Position Cognitive Cards

√ According to business mode, put different position cards on the screen.

1. Each manager has to understand the information below, including position responsibility and system, task response, and all related receipts.

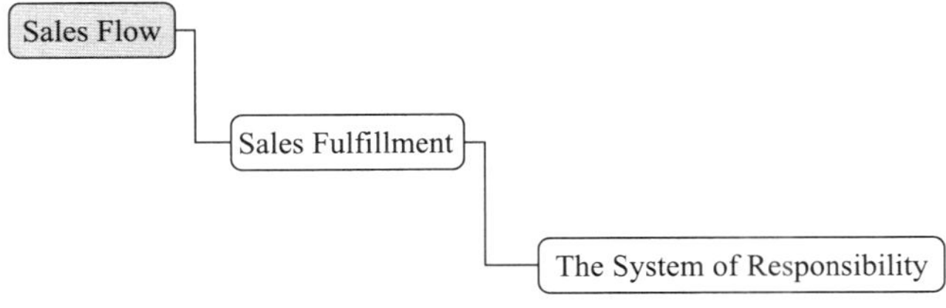

Sales Flow Chart

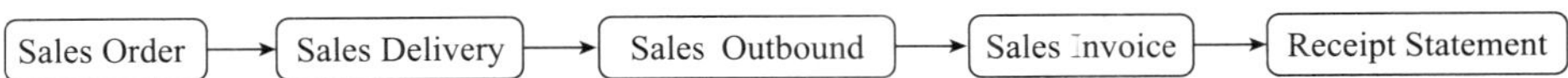

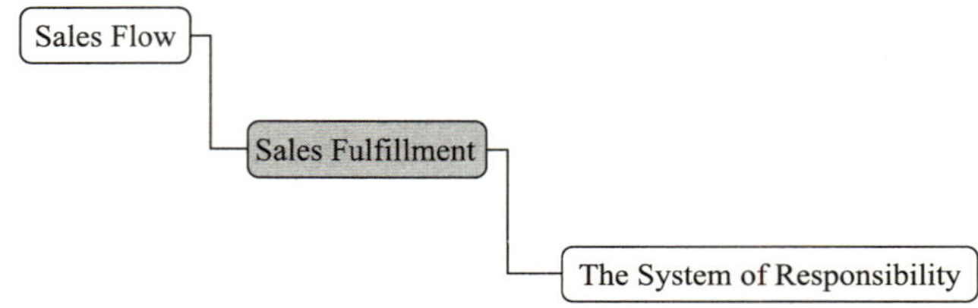

Sales Order Fulfillment Sheet

Order No.	Date	Customer	The Name of inventory	Quantity	Amount	Note
XD01	2017.04.01	Changchun Company	Comfort Baby Stroller	1,200	3,283,200,000.00	Non-finished
XD01	2017.04.01	Changchun Company	Economical Baby Stroller	2,000	5,600,000,000.00	Non-finished
XD01	2017.04.01	Changchun Company	Luxury Baby Stroller	800	2,355,200,000.00	Non-finished
XS01170302	2017.04.01	Changchun Company	Luxury Baby Stroller	1,800	11,923,200,000.00	Non-finished

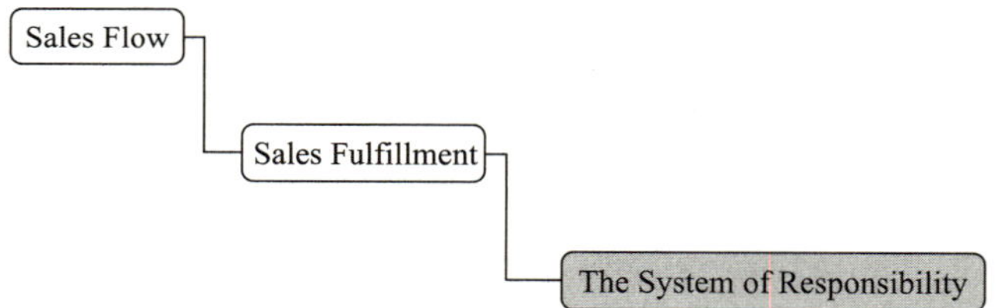

The System & Responsibility for the Sales Department

The System for the Sales Department	After receiving the sales order, the Sales Department has to communicate with the Storage Department and the Production Department, and then gives the production planning for purchasing and production
	According to the delivery sheet, the Sales Department plans the shipping of the products
	Communicate with the Financial Department to issue the sales invoice
	According to the receipt statement, pay the loans to the bank
The Responsibility for the Sales Department	Sign the sales order
	According to the order's delivery time, make the delivery planning
	According to the balance sheet, make the deliver payment planning

2. Use the position cards to check all the information, and then finish the position business receipts:

Position	Business	Name of receipt
Sales Manager	Execution of order	Sales order execution tracking sheet
Purchasing Manager		Purchasing order execution tracking sheet
Financial Manager		Account balance sheet
Production Manager	Production management and schedule work	
Storage Manager		Inventory details sheet

Subtask One: Please judge whether the following statements are correct or not, and write T (true) or F (false) in the brackets.

(1) To avoid downtime, Purchasing Manager has to purchase sales order before six days. (   )

(2) Before the payment, Purchasing Manager has to fill the fund payment plan. (   )

(3) According to production plan, Storage Manager is responsible for checking the quantity of raw materials, finished products, and semi-finished products. (   )

(4) After receiving the sales order, Sales Manager has to communicate with Production Manager and Storage Manager. (   )

(5) With raw materials and finished products into the warehouse, Storage Manager has to fill the warehouse entry sheet. (   )

(6) Financial Manager has to submit the capital planning balance sheet to the CEO on the first day of every month. (   )

(7) Financial Manager has to pay the salary on the 26th of every month. (   )

3.1.3 Enterprise Cognitive Cards

✓ Please use the enterprise cognitive cards to listen to the background, and fill in the brackets.

Dear, I will take you around our enterprise.

Firstly, we will see the enterprise layout from the left side to the right side. On the left side, the first area is our enterprise's (　　) zone, and this is the loading area.

The second area is (　　), and this is the area of product delivery.

The third area is office zone, from left to right side is the Purchasing Department, the Financial Department, and (　　).

The fourth area is raw materials storage zone and (　　). As we know, this area is for storage of the raw materials.

The fifth area is production zone: there are production lines of (　　), comfort and luxury baby strollers.

The sixth area is (　　) zone, and this area is for storage of the semi-finished products.

The seventh area is (　　) zone, for storage of the finished products temporarily.

In the production workshop of our enterprise, there are three main production lines. They are economical baby stroller, comfort baby stroller, and luxury baby stroller lines.

Among them, the production line of luxury baby stroller can produce (　　) cars each day, the production line of comfort baby stroller can produce 150 cars each day, and the production line of economical baby stroller can produce (　　) cars each day.

3.1.4 Production Operation Cards

✓ In the ARE, please try to understand the function of picking cards, finishing warehousing cards, and production execution cards.

Please finish all the questions using picking cards, finishing warehousing cards and production execution cards.

(1) Today is April 1. Use production execution card to rotate one circle forward, and then the date will change to April 2.

(2) Production execution cards of luxury baby stroller can pick up 100 pieces each time. (　　)

(3) Finishing warehousing cards of economical baby stroller can go into warehouse 100 pieces each time.

(4) Use production execution cards to finish the task, and then all the production lines will work. (　　)

(5) We can see the quantity of warehouses from the inventory e-board and data board. (　　)

Think Out of the Box

The 12 Dimensions of Business Innovation

Business guru Jim Collins's research emphasizes the importance of systematic, broad-based innovation: "Always looking for the one big breakthrough, the one big idea, is contrary to what we found: To build a truly great company, it's decision upon decision, action upon action, day upon day, month upon month... It's cumulative momentum and no one decision defines a great company." He cites the success of Walt Disney with theme parks and Walmart with retailing as examples of companies that were successful after having executed against a big idea brilliantly over such a long period of time.

Northwestern's Mohanbir Sawhney and his colleagues outline 12 dimensions of business innovation that make up the "innovation radar" (See Table 3) and suggest that business innovation is about increasing customer value, not just creating new things, comes in many flavors and can take place on any dimension of a business system; and is systematic and requires careful consideration of all aspects of a business.

Finally, to find breakthrough ideas, some companies find ways to immerse a range of employees in solving marketing problems. Samsung's Value Innovation Program (VIP) isolates product development teams of engineers, designers, and planners with a timetable and end date in the company's center just south of Seoul, Korea, while 50 specialists help guide their activities. To help make tough trade-offs, team members draw "value curves" that rank attributes such as a product's sound or picture quality on a scale from 1 to 5. To develop a new car, BMW similarly mobilizes specialists in engineering, design, production, marketing, purchasing, and finance at its Research and Innovation Center or Project House.

Table 3: The 12 Dimensions of Business Innovation

Dimension	Definition	Examples
Offerings (WHAT)	Develop innovative new products or services	✣ Gillette MACH3 Turbo Razor ✣ Apple iPod music player and iTunes music service
Platform	Use common components or building blocks to create derivative offerings	✣ General Motors OnStar telematics platform ✣ Disney animated movies
Solutions	Create integrated and customized offerings that solve end-to-end customer problems	✣ UPS logistics services Supply Chain Solutions ✣ DuPont Building Innovation for construction
Customers (WHO)	Discover unmet customer needs or identify underserved customer segments	✣ Enterprise Rent-A-Car focusing on replacement of car renters ✣ Green Mountain Energy focusing on "green power"
Customer Experience	Redesign customer interactions across all touch points and all moments of contact	✣ Washington Mutual Occasion retail banking concept ✣ Cabela's store as entertainment experience concept
Value Capture	Redefine how company gets paid or create innovative new revenue streams	✣ Google paid search ✣ Blockbuster revenue sharing with movie distributors
Process (HOW)	Redesign core operating processes to improve efficiency and effectiveness	✣ Toyota Production System for operations ✣ General Electric Design for Six Sigma (DFSS)
Organization	Change form, function, or activity scope of the firm	✣ Cisco partner-centric networked virtual organization ✣ Procter & Gamble front-back hybrid organization for customer focus

Continued

Dimension	Definition	Examples
Supply Chain	Think differently about sourcing and fulfillment	✣ Moen ProjectNet for collaborative design with suppliers ✣ General Motors Celta's use of integrated supply and online sales
Presence (WHERE)	Create new distribution channels or innovative points of presence, including the places where offerings can be bought or used by customers	✣ Starbucks music CD sales in coffee stores ✣ Diebold Remote Teller System for banking
Networking	Create network-centric intelligent and integrated offerings	✣ Otis Remote Elevator Monitoring service ✣ Department of Defense Network-Centric Warfare
Brand	Leverage a brand into new domains	✣ Virgin Group "branded venture capital" ✣ Yahoo! As a lifestyle brand

According to the 12 dimensions of business innovation, which part are you interested in?

____

____

____

____

____

____

____

____

____

____

Business Unit Strategic Planning

The business unit strategic planning process consists of the steps shown in the following chart. We examine each step in the sections that follow.

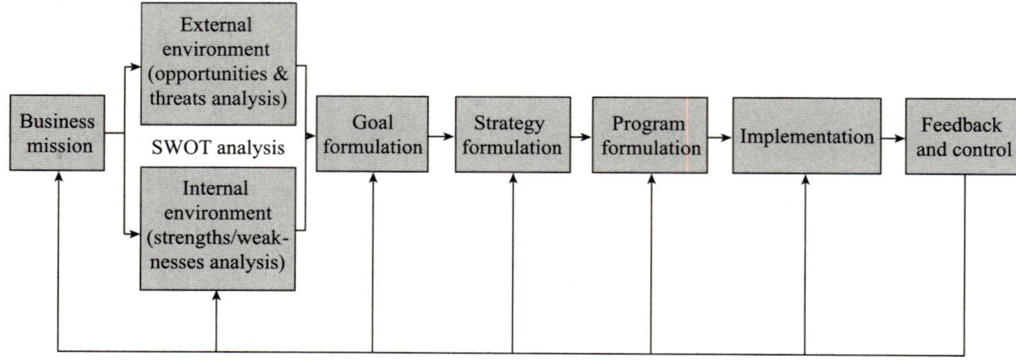

According to the business unit strategic planning, which part is the most important for you?

Expansion of Mind

The Theories about the Modern International Market Environment

Each business unit needs to define its specific mission within broader company mission. Thus, a television-studio-lighting-equipment company might define its mission as, "To target major television studios and become their vendor of choice for lighting technologies that represent the most advanced and reliable studio lighting arrangements." Notice this mission does not attempt to win business from smaller television studios, offer the lowest price, or venture into non-lighting industry.

SWOT Analysis (See Table 4)

The overall evaluation of a company's strengths, weaknesses, opportunities, and threats is called SWOT analysis. It's a way of monitoring the external and internal marketing environment.

Goal Formulation

Once the company has performed a SWOT analysis, it can proceed to goal formulation, developing specific goals for the planning period. Goals are objectives that are specific with respect to magnitude and time.

Most business units pursue a mix of objectives, including profitability, sales growth, market share improvement, risk containment, innovation, and reputation. The business units set these objectives and then manage objectives. To make an MBO (Management by Objectives) system work, the unit's objectives must meet four criteria:

◇ They must be arranged hierarchically, from most to least important;

◇ Objectives should be quantitative whenever possible;

◇ Goals should be realistic;

◇ Objectives muse be consistent.

Strategy Formulation

Goals indicate what a business unit wants to achieve; strategy is a game plan for getting there. Every business must design a strategy for achieving its goals, consisting of marketing strategy, compatible technology strategy and sourcing strategy.

Porter's Generic Strategies

Michael Porter has proposed three generic strategies that provide a good starting point for strategic thinking.

◇ Overall cost leadership: Firms work to achieve the lowest production and distribution costs so that they can underprice competitors and win market share.

◇ Differentiation: The business concentrates on achieving superior performance in an important customer benefit area valued by a large part of the market.

◇ Focus: The business focuses on one or more narrow market segments, gets to know them intimately, and pursues either cost leadership or differentiation within the target segment.

Program Formulation and Implementation

Even a great marketing strategy can be sabotaged by poor implementation. If the unit has decided to attain technological leadership, it must strengthen its R&D department, gather technological intelligence, develop leading-edge products, train its technical sales force, and communicate with its technological leadership.

Today's businessmen recognize that unless they nurture other stakeholders—customers, employees, suppliers, distributors—they may never earn sufficient profits for the stockholders. A company might aim to delight its customers, perform well for its employees, and deliver a threshold level of satisfaction to its suppliers. When setting these levels, the company can not violate any stakeholder group's benefit.

Feedback and Control

A company's strategies that fit the environment will inevitably erode, because the market environment changes faster than the company's seven Ss (strategy, structure, systems, style, skills, staffing and shared values). Thus, a company might remain efficient, yet it has lost effectiveness. Peter Drucker pointed out that it is more important to "do the right thing"—to be effective—than "to do things right"—to be efficient. The most successful companies, however, excel at both aspects.

Organizations, especially large ones, are subject to inertia. It's difficult to change one part without adjusting anything else. Yet, organizations can be changed through strong leadership, preferable in advance of a crisis. The key to organizational health is willingness to examine the changing environment and adopt new goals and behaviors.

Table 4: SWOT Analysis

Item	Internal environment	Item	External environment
Strengths	✣ Clear target customers ✣ Less competitors ✣ High-quality personnel ✣ Update information timely ✣ Strong communication ability with customers	Opportunities	✣ Policy support and entrepreneurship encouragement from the government ✣ Continual professional development ✣ Technology development and innovation ✣ Industry influences ✣ Cost advantages ✣ Local event
Weaknesses	✣ Low market share ✣ Limit budget in Research & Development ✣ Poor financial support ✣ Overly narrow product portfolio ✣ Lack of trusted partners	Threats	✣ Economic conditions ✣ More new competitors ✣ Competitors have some superiority in products or services ✣ Competitors have developed new products or services ✣ Product life cycle ✣ Decreased customer demand

According to the theories about modern international market environment, which part are you interested in?

Task Two: Understanding Enterprise

Main Content

1. Understanding the basic information of enterprise
2. Understanding the layout of enterprise
3. Understanding the structure of organization
4. Understanding the rules of operation
5. Understanding the rules of production capacity
6. Understanding the basic situation of operation

Knowledge Points

1. The layout of enterprise
2. The structure of organization
3. The rules and situation of operation
4. The rules and situation of production capacity

◇ Target of the task

1. Learning the basic information of enterprise
2. Learning the basic information of operation

3.2.1 Understanding the Background of Enterprise

Please refer to Chapter One.

3.2.2 Understanding the Layout of Enterprise

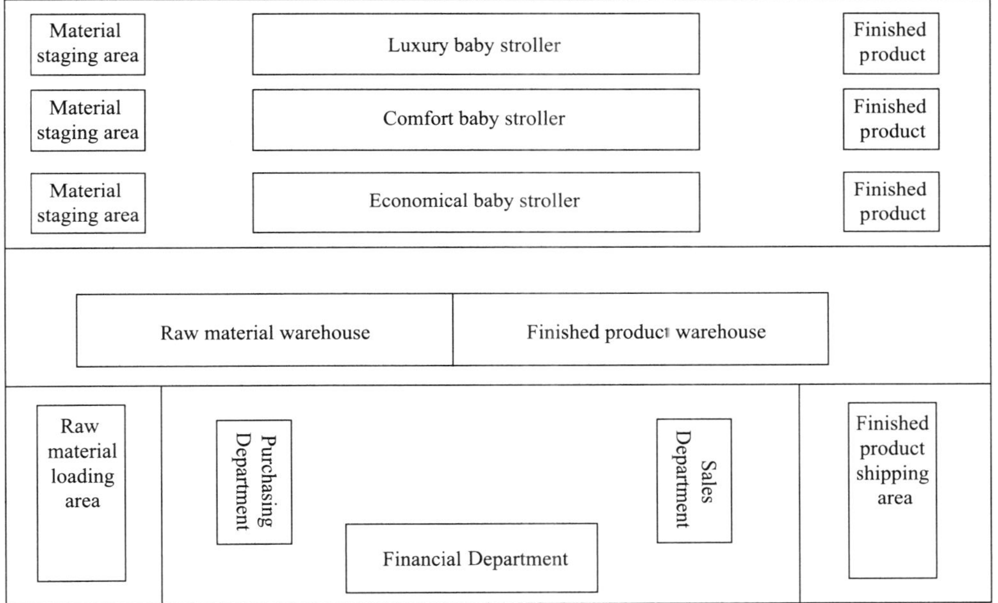

Subtask Two: Please write the answers in the brackets.

[Using the cards] Finish all the topics.

(1) In the stock area of ARE screen, there is/are ( ) kind(s) of raw materials in the status bar.

(2) In the Financial Department of ARE screen, there is/are ( ), loans and receivables as well as a ( ).

(3) Pure cotton cushion is in the ( ) position of raw material warehouse.

(4) Comfort baby stroller is in the ( ) position of finished product

warehouse.

(5) On the e-board of raw materials, we can check the warehouse of the highest capacity of numerical control chips. (   )

(6) In the finished product warehouse, there are economical baby strollers, comfort baby strollers and luxury baby strollers. Pay more attention to the quantity of warehouses, and the largest inventory is (   ).

(7) In the production workshop, there is a cultural wall about 6S management, that is, SEIRI, (   ), SEISO, (   ), SEIKETSU and (   ).

(8) Check the data of warehouse of raw materials. (Finishing/Finished)

(9) Check the data of warehouse of finished products. (Finishing/Finished)

(10) Check the storage of temporary products. (Finishing/Finished)

(11) Check the e-board of warehouse of the material staging area. (Finishing/Finished)

3.2.3 Understanding the Structure of Organization

✓ Please understand the structure of organization.

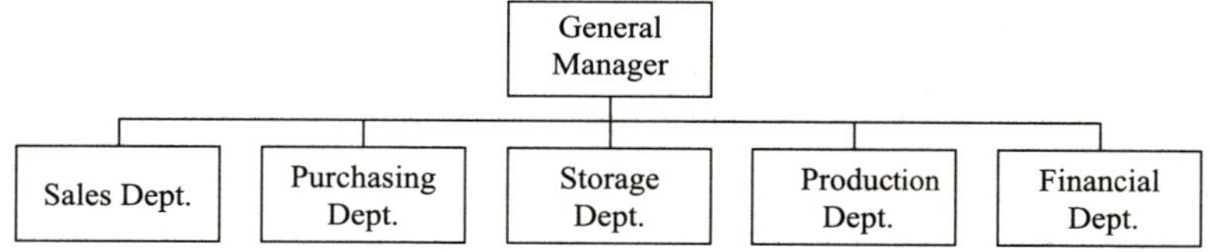

3.2.4 Understanding the Rules of Operation

✓ Please use the position cards and case study in the teaching platform to finish the following sentences.

1. The rules of the position of Financial Manager:

1) Submit the capital planning balance sheet on the (   ) (date) of each month to CEO.

2) According to the application sheet of capital payment, the Financial Department can pay the money on the (   ) (date) of each month.

3) Pay the salary on the (   ) (date) of each month.

2. The rules of the position of Production Manager:

1) According to the production order, Production Manager has to manage the raw materials, in order to avoid more inventories in the workshop.

2) Do (   ) formalities on time after products have been produced.

3) According to the plan of product, Production Manager has to fill up the schedule of raw material demand in order to prohibit false declaration, overstatement, and concealment.

3. The rules of the position of Purchasing Manager:

1) According to the purchasing order, pay before (   ) days, in order to avoid downtime.

2) Before the payment for goods, Purchasing Manager has to receive products, check products and put them into storage.

3) Take long-term capital plan in order to avoid wasting capital.

4. The rules of the position of Sales Manager:

1) After accepting the sales order, Sales Manager has to communicate with the Storage Department and the Production Department, and then submit (   ) and purchasing plan to the Purchasing Department.

2) According to the sales order, deliver goods on time.

3) Cooperate with the Financial Department, and submit (   ).

4) According to the date, collect payment for goods on time.

5. The rules of the position of Storage Manager:

1) Storage Manager has to check the raw materials and inventory and fill up (   ) and (   ).

2) According to (   ), arrange the outbound raw materials and fill up the outbound sheet of raw materials.

3) According to (   ), arrange the outbound products and fill up the outbound

sheet of products.

4) According to the sales sheet, arrange the outbound products and fill up (   ).

3.2.5 Understanding the Rules of Production Capacity

✓ Please check the background of the rules of production capacity of the enterprise or use information of the production execution card in ARE to finish the questions.

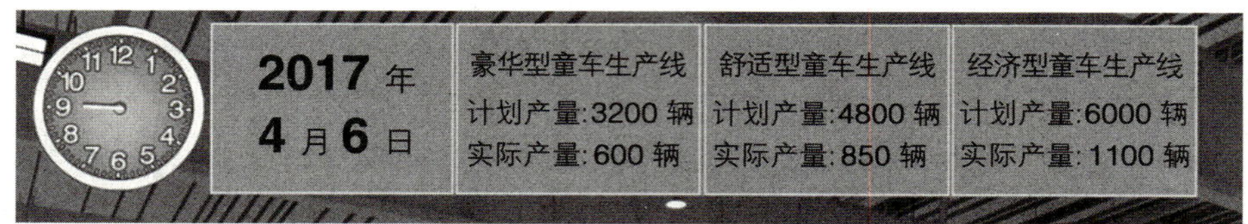

1) From the angle of business logic, Production Manager will give sales order information to Sales Manager. (T/F)

2) From the angle of business logic, Production Manager communicates with Storage Manager on time. (T/F)

3) Picking fewer materials will affect production more than picking more materials. (T/F)

4) After products have been finished, Storage Manager, rather than Production Manager, will deal with the paper work about warehouse. (T/F)

5) The Production Department only needs to focus on the maximum production capacity of the production line, and doesn't need to pay more attention to planning. (T/F)

6) In fact, production order will be supervised on time. (T/F)

7) Each production line is different. (T/F)

8) Using production execution cards, we can only know the demand of product. (T/F)

3.2.6 Understanding the Basic Situation of Operation

✓ Please check the enterprise situation in Appendix 1, and finish all the following questions.

1) In the initial balance sheet, gross of accounts receivable is________________.

2) In the initial inventory purchasing price list, chip's unit price (tax included) is ____.

3) In the supplier inventory price list, space cotton's unit price is____________________________.

4) In the initial finished product list, the quantity of luxury baby stroller is ____.

5) In the initial inventory purchasing price list, the purchasing cost of luxury baby stroller is____________________________________.

6) In the initial inventory purchasing price list, economical baby stroller's unit price (tax included) is________________________________.

7) In the supplier inventory price list, each product only has one supplier. (T/F)

8) In the supplier inventory price list, each supplier can only provide one material. (T/F)

9) In the initial payroll payable, salary has to include five kinds of social insurance and housing provident fund. (T/F)

10) According to the relationship between cost and product price, the highest profit rate belongs to luxury baby stroller. (T/F)

Think Out of the Box

Social Research

Please choose three companies, and then answer the following questions respectively:

1. What's the origin of the company's name?

2. Does the company's name bring good business benefits?

3. Would CEO change the company's name easily?

The Basic Information about Setting up a Business

If you would like to set up a new business, you have to choose a suitable way to start your company. If you choose a right way, you will get a better chance to success. According to the real situation, several principles were introduced as follows:

1. Common ways for college students to start their own business:

✓ Acquisition of existing enterprises

✓ Franchisee

✓ Technology entrepreneurship

✓ Internet entrepreneurship

✓ Part-time entrepreneurship

✓ Competition entrepreneurship

✓ Innovation entrepreneurship

2. Common principles for college students to select their own business:

✓ According to their own specialty

✓ According to their own interest

✓ According to their own capital ability

✓ According to their own capital support

✓ According to their own channel

3. Choose the direction of setting up a business.

4. Design the purpose of setting up a business.

5. Select the industry of setting up a business.

6. Create the environment of setting up a business.

7. Analyze the condition of setting up a business.

8. Have a keen sense of business and care for the market.

9. Dare to challenge yourself.

10. Have team consciousness.

11. Have a sense of responsibility.

Question: Under the leadership of the CEO, please discuss the details about the process of setting up a business. If you have to set up a business, what else do you think you have to prepare?

Expansion of Mind

Table 5: Corporate Social Initiatives

Type	Description	Example
Corporate social marketing	Supporting behavior change campaigns	McDonald's promotion of a statewide childhood immunization campaign in Oklahoma
Cause marketing	Promoting social issues through efforts such as sponsorships, licensing agreements, and advertising	McDonald's sponsorship of Forest (a gorilla) at Sydney's Zoo—a 10-year sponsorship commitment, aiming at preserving this endangered species
Cause-related marketing	Donating a percentage of revenues to a specific cause based on the revenue occurring during the announced period of support	McDonald's earmarking of $1 for Ronald McDonald Children's Charities from the sale of every Big Mac and pizza sold on McHappy Day
Corporate philanthropy	Making gifts of money, goods, or time to help nonprofit organizations, groups, or individuals	McDonald's contributions to Ronald McDonald House Charities
Corporate community involvement	Providing in-kind or volunteer services in the community	McDonald's catering meals for firefighters in the December 1997 bushfires in Australia
Socially responsible business practices	Adopting and conducting business practices that protect the environment and human and animal rights	McDonald's requirement that suppliers increase the amount of living space for laying hens on factory farms

Table 6: Some Examples of Master Marketers

Amazon.com	Electrolux	Progressive Insurance
Band & Olufsen	Enterprise Rent-A-Car	Ritz-Carlton
Barnes & Noble	Google	Samsung
Best Buy	Harley-Davidson	Sony
BMW	Honda	Southwest Airlines
Borders	IKEA	Starbuck's
Canon	LEGO	Target
Caterpillar	McDonald's	Tesco
Club Med	Nike	Toyota
Costco	Nokia	Virgin
Disney	Nordstorm	Walmart
eBay	Procter & Gamble	Whole Foods

Task Three: Understanding Basic Business

Main Content

1. Understanding basic information of business system
2. Understanding business flow of enterprise
3. Understanding the raw material list
4. Understanding and drawing logistics flow chart
5. Understanding and drawing enterprise information flow chart
6. Understanding and drawing enterprise capital flow chart

Knowledge Points

1. Enterprise business system
2. Enterprise business flow
3. List of raw materials
4. Enterprise logistics flow
5. Enterprise information flow
6. Enterprise capital flow

◇ Target of the task

1. Learning basic business system
2. Learning basic capital flow system

3.3.1 Understanding Business System

√ Please understand all information about the position. This is the most important step to understand the whole enterprise. (See Chapter One)

3.3.2 Understanding Enterprise Business Flow

√ Please login each manager card to understand the business flows of different positions

Position	Basic rules that other positions have to know
Financial Manager	Submit a capital planning balance sheet to CEO on the first day of each month
Production Manager	
Sales Manager	
Purchasing Manager	
Storage Manager	

Subtask Three: Fill in the following flow charts.

a) Financial flow

Flow 1: Payment flow (including General Manager approval, payment application sheet, capital transfer sheet, accounting voucher, and capital planning)

[ ] → [ ] → [ ] → [ ] → [ ]

Flow 2: Gathering flow (including Bank statement, accounting voucher, filling up receipt, and sending goods)

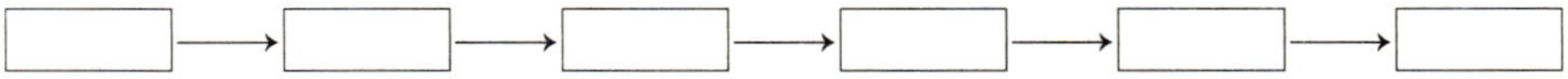

[ ] → [ ] → [ ] → [ ] → [ ] → [ ]

Flow 3: Monthly statement flow (including production cost settlement, business reconciliation, bookkeeping, reconciliation, and loss and gain brought forward)

[ ] → [ ] → [ ] → [ ] → [ ]

b) Purchasing flow

Flow 1: Standard procurement (including purchasing planning, purchasing IM-warehouse, payment, verification, purchasing order, and purchasing arrival sheet)

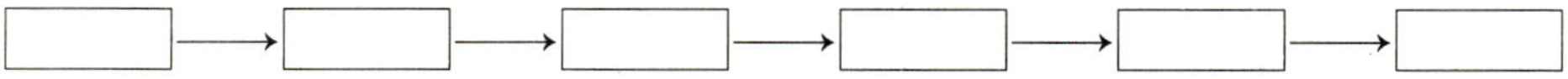

[ ] → [ ] → [ ] → [ ] → [ ] → [ ]

Flow 2: Payment flow (including capital planning, purchasing bill, payment sheet, verification, and payment application sheet)

[ ] → [ ] → [ ] → [ ] → [ ]

c) Sales flow

Sales flow: (including sales EX-warehouse, sales bill, verification, receipt, sales shipment, and sales order)

[ ] → [ ] → [ ] → [ ] → [ ] → [ ]

d) Storage flow

Flow 1: (including quality check list, raw material IM-warehouse sheet, and purchasing order notice sheet)

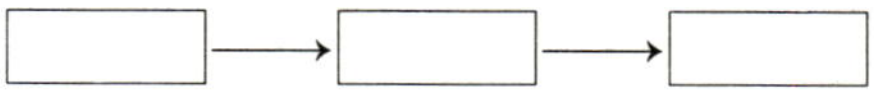

[ ] → [ ] → [ ]

Flow 2: (including raw material EX-warehouse, raw material IM-warehouse, and picking list)

Flow 3: (including product IM-warehouse, finished product IM-warehouse, and finished work report sheet)

Flow 4: (including sales sending sheet, sales EX-warehouse, and sales put-out-storage)

e) Producing flow

Producing flow: (including sales order, finished goods IM-warehouse, production planning, finished work report sheet, production execution, and production order)

3.3.3 Understanding Raw Materials

✓ Please use BOM cards to fill in the blanks.

a) Raw materials list for economical baby stroller

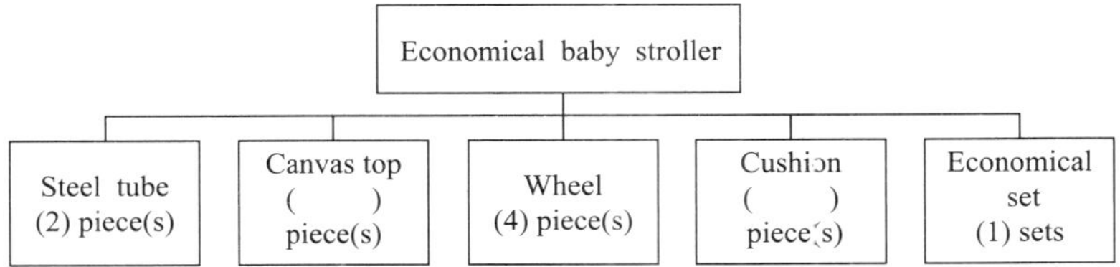

b) Raw materials list for comfort baby stroller

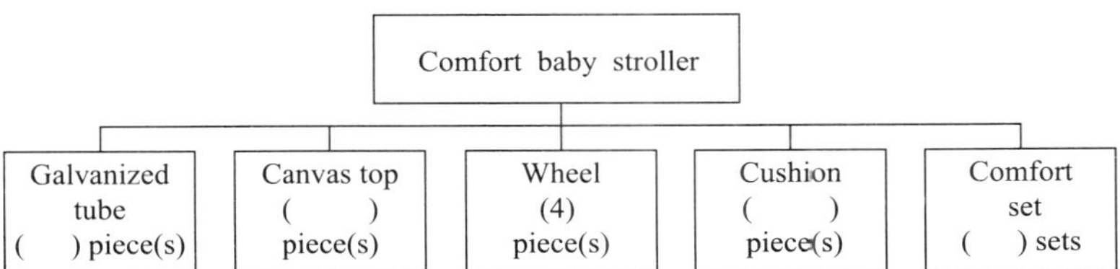

c) Raw material list for luxury baby stroller

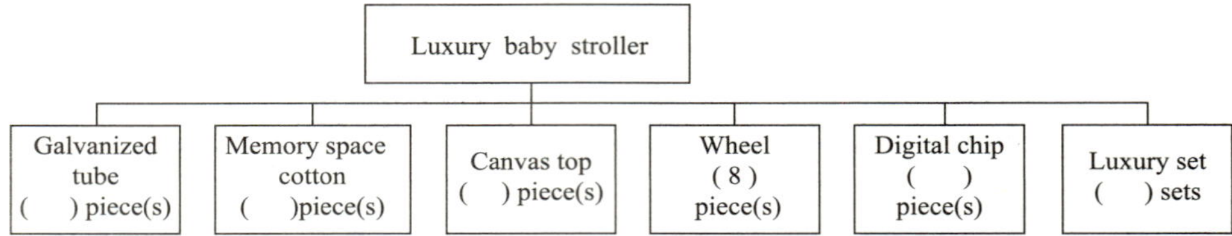

✓ Please finish the following questions.

1. Luxury baby stroller's wheel, canvas top and galvanized tube are the same with other baby strollers' wheel, canvas top and galvanized tube. (T/F)

2. ( ) galvanized tube is purchased when producing 500 comfort baby strollers.

3. When purchasing raw materials, those raw materials should arrive within ( ) day(s).

3.3.4 Understanding Enterprise Logistics Process

✓ Please look at enterprise logistics flow chart below, and then finish the following wiring questions.

a) Look at enterprise logistics flow chart.

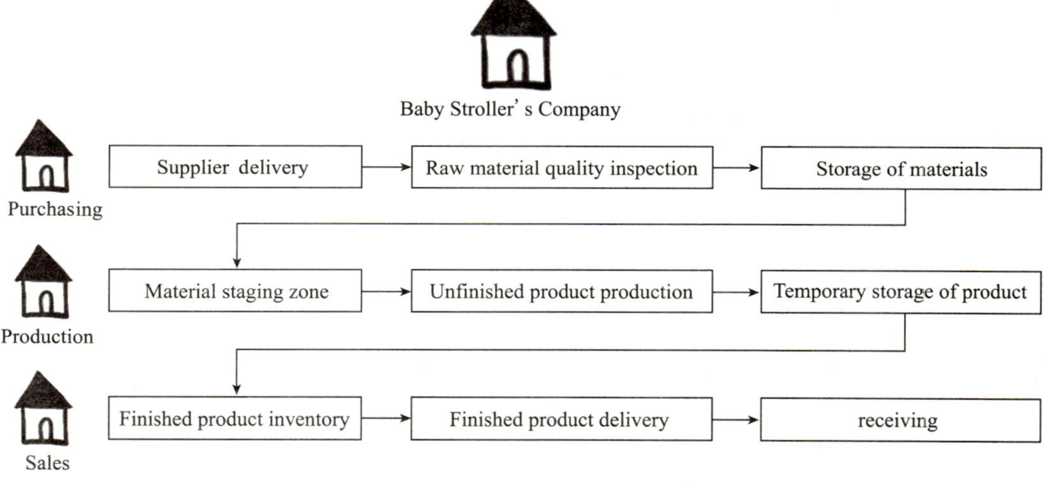

b) Draw lines to connect different departments in the chart.

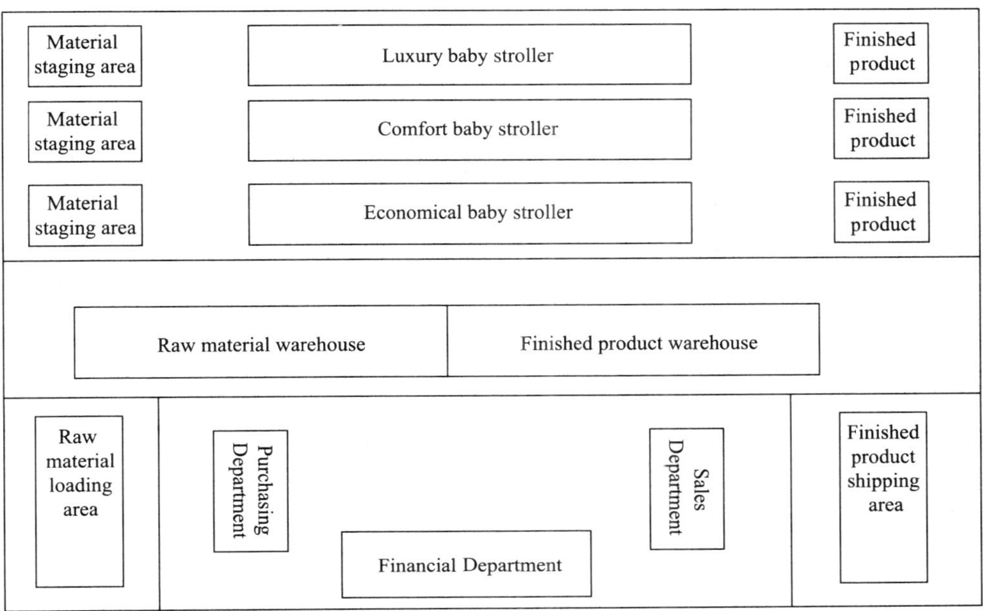

3.3.5 Understanding Enterprise Information Flow

✓ Please look at enterprise information flow chart below, and then finish the following wiring questions.

a) Look at enterprise information flow chart.

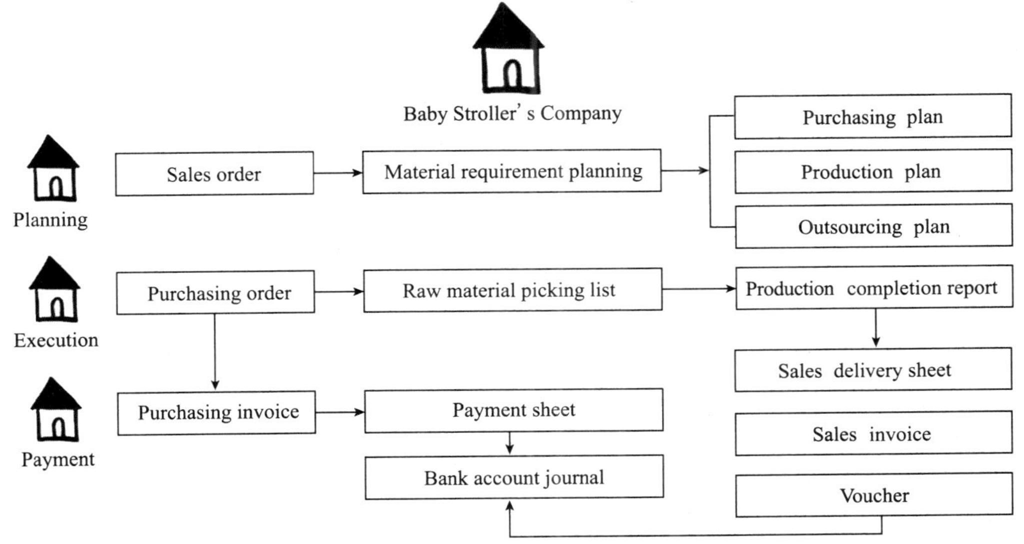

b) Draw lines to connect different departments in the chart.

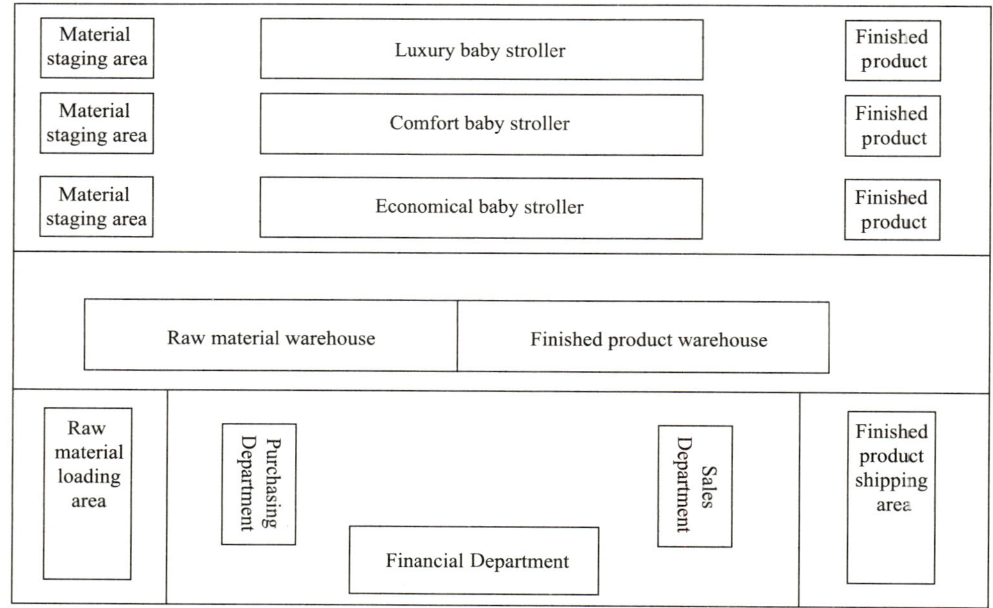

3.3.6 Understanding Enterprise Capital Flow

✓ Please look at enterprise capital flow chart below, and then finish the following wiring questions.

a) Look at enterprise capital flow chart.

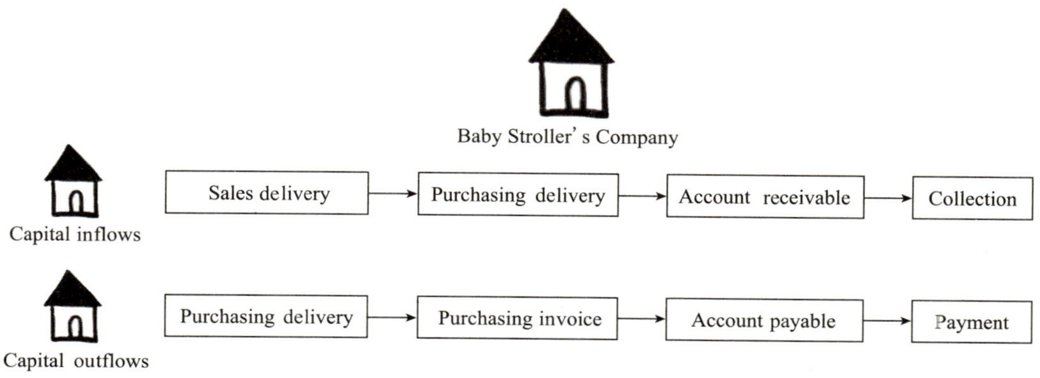

a) Draw lines to connect different departments in the chart.

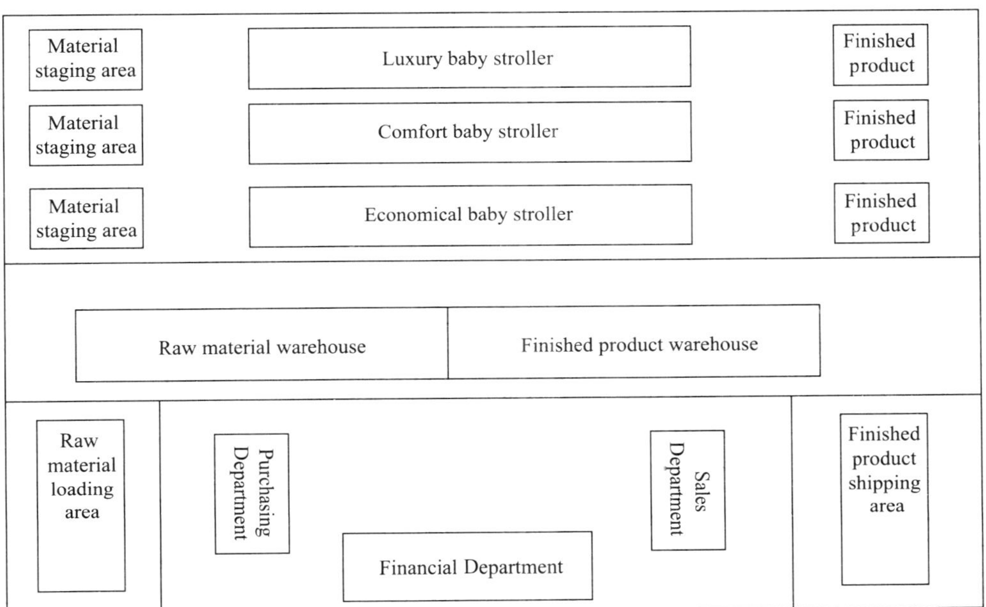

Think Out of the Box

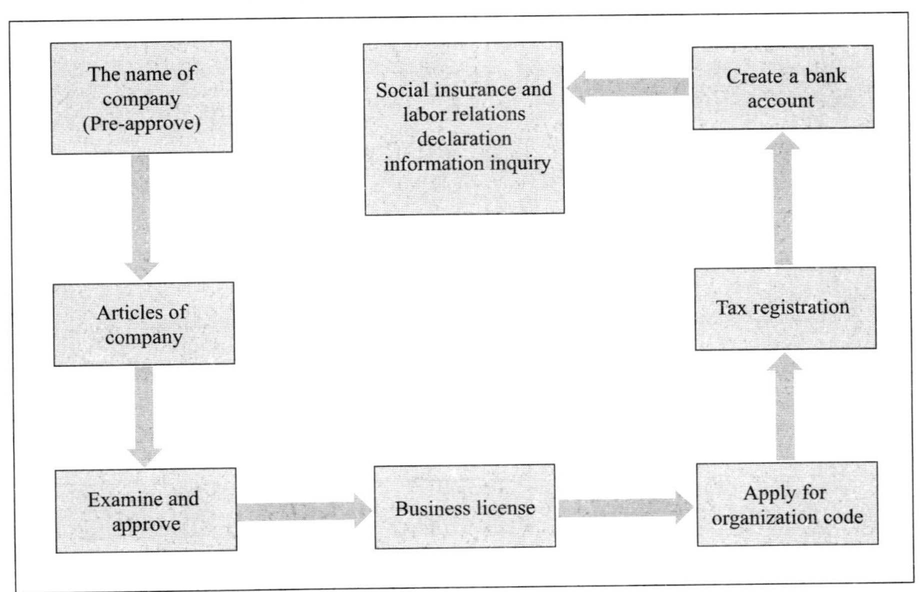

According to the chart above, write down your ideas:

____

____

____

____

____

____

____

____

The Strategic Planning, Implementation and Control Processes

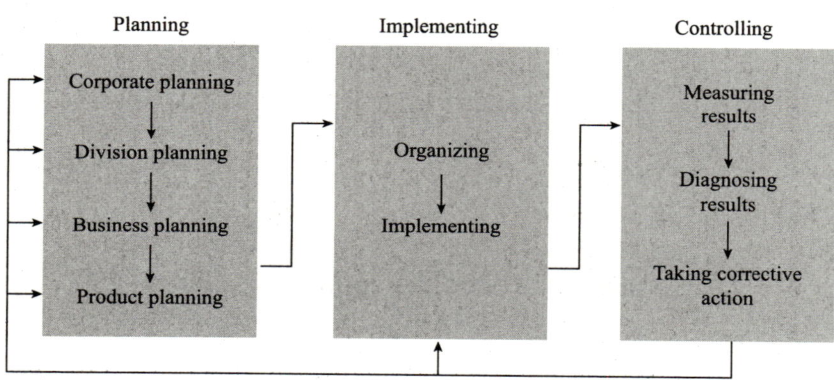

Combine with ARE and the chart of strategic planning, implementation and control processes, write down your ideas:

____

____

____

____

____

____

____

Task Four: Understanding Basic Position Information

Main Content

1. Understanding the responsibility of position
2. Understanding and drawing the position flow
3. Setting the report of position
4. Understanding the sheet of position
5. Understanding the data of position

Knowledge Points

1. The responsibility of position
2. The position flow
3. The reports and sheets of position
4. The data of position

◇ Target of the task

1. Learning the basic responsibility of position
2. Learning the basic flow of position

3.4.1 Understanding the Responsibility of Position

Subtask Four: Please understand the responsibility of position, and then finish the following questions.

1. The responsibility of Financial Manager is: (keyword)

1) To collect each department's ( ), and according to sales returned money planning to write ( ).

2) Based on a daily business, Financial Manager makes ( ) on time.

3) To pay the salary.

4) To make capital balance sheet and profit sheet.

5) To write purchase invoice and submit it to ( ).

2. The responsibility of Production Manager is: (keyword)

1) According to sales order, to make production planning and make sure all the work is done on time.

2) According to production planning, to make ( ).

3) To cooperate with the Storage Department and put finished products into the warehouse on time.

4) To maintain equipment.

3. The responsibility of Sales Manager is: (keyword)

1) Sign in ( ).

2) According to ship time of sales order, to make ( ) in order to arrange the car on time.

3) According to the capital payment balance sheet to plan the transportation charge.

4) To cooperate with Financial Department, and write ( ) on time.

4. The responsibility of Purchasing Manager is: (keyword)

1) To plan ( ) according to MPS/MRP.

2) To ask price first, and then ensure supplier and ( ).

3) To fill in the in voice and ( ), and then submit them to the Financial Department to register account payable.

4) To write down ( ) and give it/them to the supplier.

5) To deal with the problem of quality.

5. The responsibility of Storage Manager is: (keyword)

1) To check raw material, IM-warehouse, and write down ( ) and ( ).

2) According to the ( ) plan, to fill in the raw material EX-warehouse sheet.

3) According to the ( ) plan, to fill in the finished product IM-warehouse.

4) According to the sales shipping order plan, fill in the ( ).

Subtask Five: Test.

1) Storage Manager's main assignment is managing the IM-warehouse & EX-warehouse. (T/F)

2) In the finished product warehouse, the highest capacity for all the economical, comfort and luxury baby strollers is 10,000 pieces. (T/F)

3) Space cotton cushion is put in A01. (T/F)

4) In the raw material warehouse, the safety stock of all kinds of raw materials is 100 pieces. (F/T)

5) MPS is the acronym for ( ), meaning ( ).

6) MRP is the acronym for ( ), meaning ( ).

3.4.2 Understanding the Position's Flow

✓ Please look at the following enterprise information flow chart.

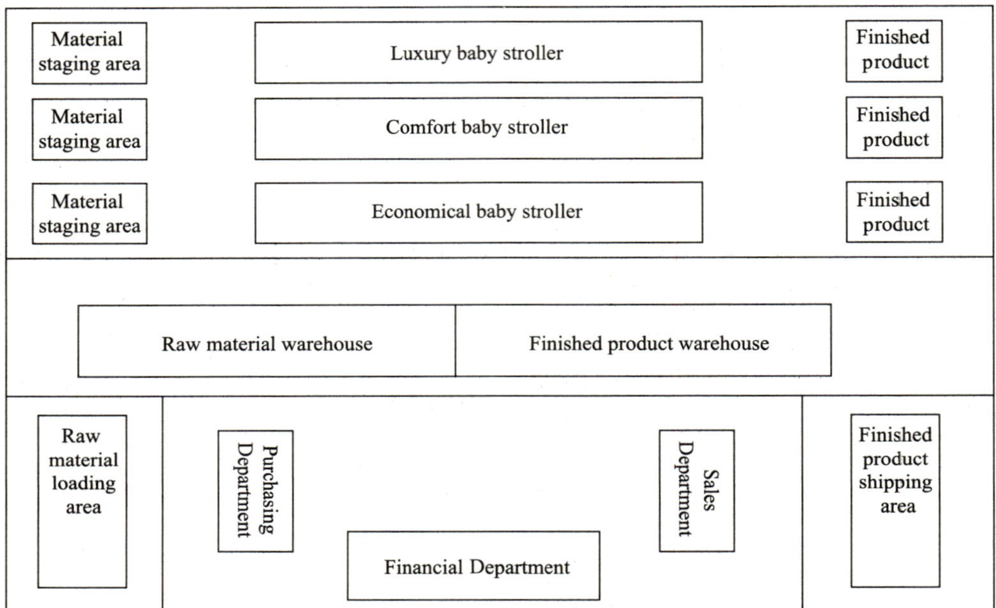

3.4.3 Understanding the Position's Report

✓ Please use General Manager cards to finish the following six reports.

Report name	Keywords	Position
Profit sheet	Income, profit, net profit	
Capital balance sheet		
Asset occupancy list		
Bank statement book		
Account payable ledger		
Account receivable ledger		

Subtask Six: Please finish the following questions.

1) General Manager asks what kind of money needs to pay in the next month. (Y/N)

2) General Manager asks how much money will be collected in the next month. (Y/N)

3) General Manager asks how many business transactions' amount is more than 500,000 yuan in the last month. (Y/N)

4) General Manager asks the balance of the beginning of April. (Y/N)

5) General Manager asks the proportion of the financial cost. (Y/N)

6) General Manager asks how much VAT is paid in the last month. (Y/N)

7) General Manager asks the details of income and cost. (Y/N)

3.4.4 Understanding Position Sheets

✓ Please use the position card to look for related information.

Name	Related Sheets
General Manager	
Financial Manager	
Sales Manager	
Purchasing Manager	
Storage Manager	

3.4.5 Understanding Position Data

Subtask Seven: Please check initial data in Appendix 1, look for the position's data and mark them on the following chart.

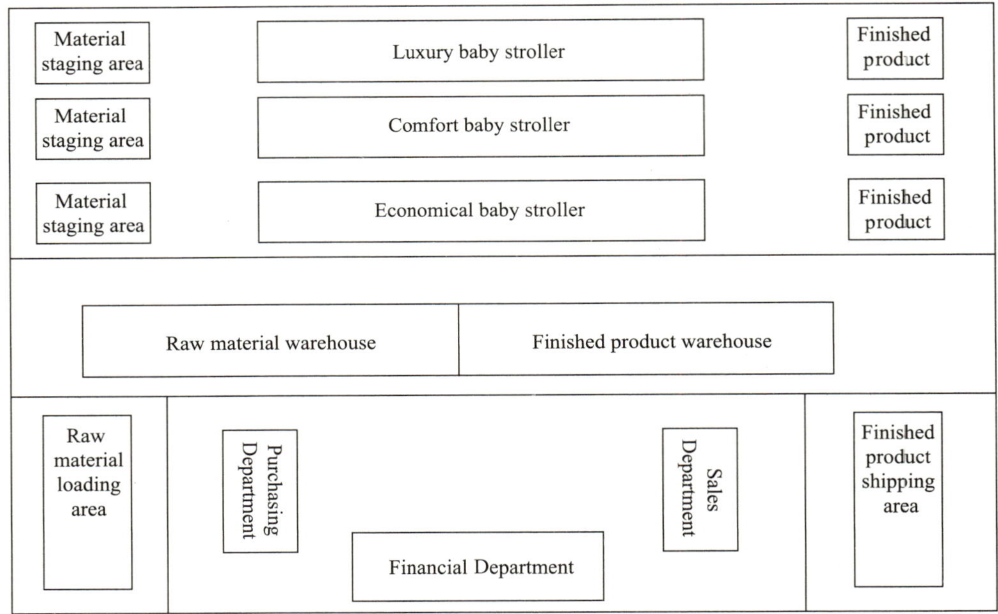

1. Each position's information

Discuss the questions below, and then think about which position should answer the question. Make sure to choose the position first, and then answer the question.

1) General Manager: Now, how many economical baby strollers, comfort baby strollers, and luxury baby strollers can be supported by raw materials in our storage?

Management responsibility/answer:

2) General Manager: What kinds of incomes are there in April? What kinds of outcomes are there in April?

Management responsibility/answer:

3) General Manager: What kinds of sales order do we need to pay in April?

How many products do we need to produce at least?

Management responsibility/answer:

4) General Manager: What about sales volume about all kinds of products in March? Could you forecast it in next month?

Management responsibility/answer:

2. Each position's information

1) General Manager: If all production lines run at full production capability in April, how many products can we produce?

Management responsibility/answer:

2) General Manager: From now to 1st April, does material staging area still keep the raw materials?

Management responsibility/answer:

3) General Manager: Please tell me if you can forecast the income and outcome in next month? can we have a capital risk?

Management responsibility/answer:

4) General Manager: How many products can we produce until the end of April?

Management responsibility/answer:

Think Out of the Box

Table 7: Competitive Territory and Boundaries in Mission Statements

Industry. Some companies operate in only one industry; some only in a set of related industries. ✣ Caterpillar focuses on the industrial market; John Deere operates in the industrial and consumer markets.
Products and applications. Firms usually define the range of products and applications they will supply. ✣ St.Jude Medical is "dedicated to developing medical technology and services that put more control in the hands of physicians, and that advance the practice of medicine and contribute to successful outcomes for every patient."
Competence. The firm identifies the range of technological and other core competencies it will master and leverage. ✣ Japan's NEC has built its core competencies in computing, communications, and components to support production of laptop computers, television receivers, and handheld telephones.
Market segment. The type of market or customers a company will serve is market segment. ✣ Aston Martin makes only high-performance sports cars. Gerber serves primarily the baby market.
Vertical comparison. The vertical sphere is the number of channel levels, from raw material to final product and distribution, in which a company will participate. ✣ At one extreme are companies with a large vertical scope. American Apparel dyes, designs, sews, markets, and distributes its line of clothing apparel out of a single building in downtown Los Angeles. ✣ At the other extreme are "hollow corporations," which outsource the production of nearly all goods and services to suppliers. Metro International prints 34 free local newspaper editions in 16 countries. It employs few reporters and owns no printing processes; instead it purchases its articles from other news sources and outsources all printing and much of its distribution to third parties.
Geographical analysis. The range of regions, countries, or country groups in which a company will operate defines its geographical sphere. ✣ Some companies operate in a specific site or state. Others are multinationals like Deutsche Post DHL and Royal Dutch Shell, which operate in more than 100 countries.

According to Table 7, what kind of opinions do you have?

____

____

____

Expansion of Mind

The Marketing Research Process

Step 1: Define the problem, the decision alternatives, and the research objectives

Step 2: Develop the research plan

✓ Data sources

✓ Research approaches

✓ Survey research

✓ Behavioral research

✓ Experimental research

✓ Research instruments

✓ Sampling plan

✓ Number of local vehicles

Step 3: Collect the information

Step 4: Analyze the information

Step 5: Present the findings

Step 6: Make the decision

Table 8：Major Consumer Promotion Tools

Major Consumer Promotion Tools
Samples：Offer of a product or service delivered door–to–door，sent in the mail，picked up in a store，attached to another product.
Coupons：Certificates entitling the bearer to a stated saving on the purchase of a specific product：mailed，enclosed in other products or attached to them，or inserted in magazine and newspaper ads.
Cash refunds（rebates）：Providing a price reduction after purchase rather than at the retail shop：Consumer sends a specified "proof of purchase" to the manufacturer，who "refunds" part of the purchase price by mail.
Price packs（cents–off deals）：Providing a lower price of a product，which is usually flagged on the label or package. A reduced–price pack is a single package sold at a reduced price（such as two for the price one）. A banded pack is two related products banded together（such as a toothbrush and toothpaste）.
Premiums（gifts）：Merchandise offered at a relatively low cost or free as an incentive to purchase a particular product. A with–pack premium accompanies the product inside or on the package. A free in–the–mail premium is mailed to the consumer who has sent a proof of purchase，such as a box top or UPC code. A self–liquidating premium is sold below its normal retail price to the consumer who requests it.
Frequency programs：Programs providing rewards related to the consumer's frequency and intensity in purchasing the company's products or services.
Prizes（contests，sweepstakes，and games）：Prizes are offers of the chance to win cash，trips，or merchandise as a result of purchasing something. A contest calls for consumers to submit an entry to be examined by a panel of judges，who will select the best entries. A sweepstake asks consumers to submit their names in a drawing. A game presents consumers with something every time they buy—bingo numbers，missing letters—which might help them win a prize.
Patronage awards：Values in cash or in other forms that are proportional to the patronage of a certain vendor or group of vendors.
Free trials：Inviting prospective purchasers to try the product without cost in the hope that they will buy.
Product warranties：Explicit or implicit promises by the seller that the product will perform as specified；otherwise，that the seller will fix it or refund the customer's money during a specified period.
Tie–in promotions：Two or more brands or companies team up on coupons，refunds，and contests to increase pulling power.
Cross–promotions：Using one brand to advertise another uncompetitive brand.
Point–of–purchase（P–O–P）Displays and Demonstrations：P–O–P displays and demonstrations take place at the point of purchase or sales.

Chapter Four

Business Cognition

Task One: Collaboration of Production and Sales

Main Content

1. Understanding the collaboration of production and sales
2. Understanding how to match the receipts and the steps on the screen
3. Practicing to make connection with production and marketing

Knowledge Points

1. The collaboration of production and sales
2. The receipts
3. The position's bill
4. Basic Chinese production–marketing receipts

◇ Target of the task

1. Learning basic information of the collaboration of production and sales
2. Preliminarily understanding the Chinese receipts

4.1.1 Understanding the Collaboration of Production and Sales

✓Please take all the orders one by one in order to understand the business receipts.

A. Finished warehouse-in

B. Sales warehouse-out

C. Sales order

D. Financial settlement

E. Production planning

F. Picking material for production

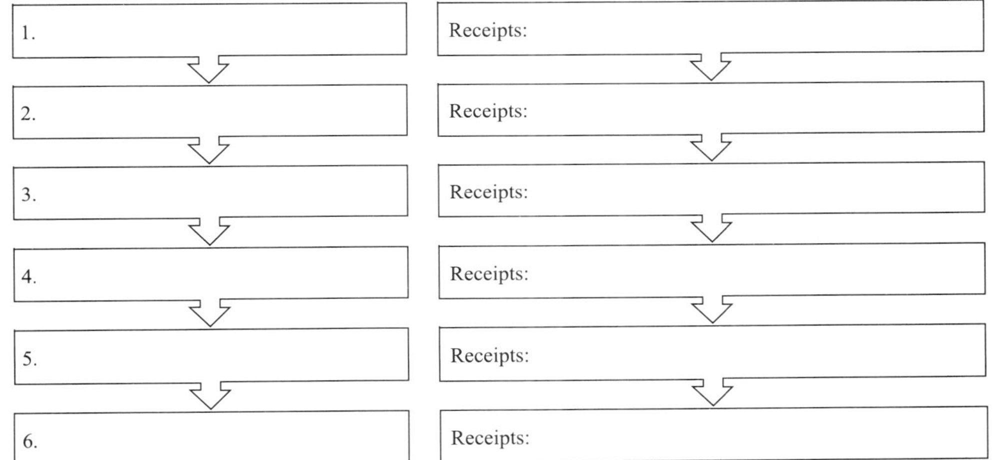

4.1.2 Real Situation Matching with Business Receipts

Subtask One: Please write down the name of receipts on the sticky note, then put the sticky note on the cognition screen.

✓Example: write down the "Finished work report"on the finished product area.

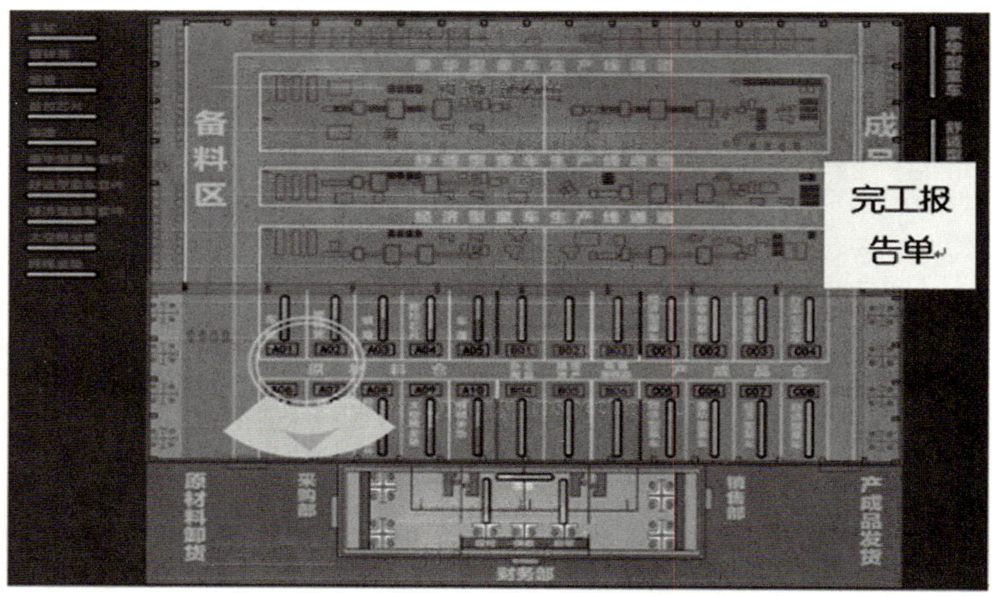

4.1.3 Practicing Collaboration of Production and Sales

Subtask Two: According to the screen of production-marketing coordination in ARE, please write down main assignments about the receipts on the table.

Step name	Receipt	Position	Notes
Sales order	Sales order sheet	Sales Manager	Customer name, drawer name, quantity, deadline

4.1.4 Summarizing the Value of Collaboration of Production and Sales

Subtask Three: Please recall the flow of production-marketing coordination, and think about the value of production-marketing coordination.

1. What is the meaning of the receipts?

2. What is the meaning of the position?

3. What is the meaning of the flow?

4. What is the meaning of the enterprise management?

4.1.5 Preliminary Understanding of Basic Chinese Receipts (Sample Only)

启明星童车有限公司

№　65628833

客户名称：华晨童车商贸有限公司　　**销 售 订 单**　　销售合同编号：110223412

订单编号：110201704010010　　制单日期：2017年 4 月1 日

序号	品名	最迟交货时间	单位	数量	含税单价	金额	备注
1	豪华型童车	4月10日	辆	500	3680	1840000	
2							
3							
4							
5							
金额合计	大写	人民币壹佰捌拾肆万元整			小写	1840000	

销售：罗雲　生产：萧侥　仓储：王储　经办：

①客户　②销售　③仓储

新道教〔2017〕ARE201号北京印刷有限公司

Receipt 1: Sales Order

启明星童车有限公司

№ 59865678

生产排产单

编号：2017040101　　　　生产线：豪华型

序号	销售订单编号	品名	单位	生产数量	交货日期	备注
1	110201704010010	豪华型童车	辆	400	2017/4/10	
2						
3						
4						
5						
6						
7						
				400		

生产：萧侥　　　　经办：张齐玲

新通教〔2017〕ARE201号北京印刷有限公司

①生产 ②仓库 ③存根

Receipt 2: Production Scheduling Sheet

启明星童车有限公司

№ 65465135

物料需求清单

部门：生产部　　　　制单日期：2017年4月1日

序号	名称	规格型号	单位	需求数量	需求日期	采购补货日期	备注
1	车轮	Φ200*Φ125/H30mm	个	3200	4月1日		
2	镀锌管	Φ18*Φ15/L1000mm	根	800	4月1日		
3	钢管	Φ18*Φ15/L1000mm	根				
4	数控芯片	MCX3154A	片	400	4月1日		
5	车篷	HJ72*32*40	个	400	4月1日		
6	豪华型童车套件	HJTB100	套	400	4月1日		
7	舒适型童车套件	HJTB200	套				
8	经济型童车套件	HJTB300	套				
9	纯棉坐垫	JHM500	件				
10	太空棉坐垫	JHM600	件	400	4月1日		
用途							

仓储：王储　　生产：萧侥　　采购：李响　　经办：

新通教〔2017〕ARE303号北京印刷有限公司

①仓储 ②采购 ③生产

Receipt 3: Material Demand List

启明星童车有限公司

领 料 单

№ 65465199

部门：生产部　　　　制单日期：2017年4月1日

序号	名称	规格型号	单位	申领数量	实发数量	退库数量	备注
1	车轮	Φ200*Φ125/H30mm	个	3200	3200		
2	镀锌管	Φ18*Φ15/L1000mm	根	800	800		
3	钢管	Φ18*Φ15/L1000mm	根				
4	数控芯片	MCX3154A	片	400	400		
5	车篷	HJ72*32*40	个	400	400		
6	豪华型童车套件	HJTB100	套	400	400		
7	舒适型童车套件	HJTB200	套				
8	经济型童车套件	HJTB300	套				
9	纯棉坐垫	JHM500	件				
10	太空棉坐垫	JHM600	件	400	400		
用途	按订单生产						

生产：萧侥　　仓储：王储　　经办：

新通教〔2017〕ARE303号北京印刷有限公司

①生产 ②仓储 ③记账

Receipt 4: Picking List

启明星童车有限公司

出 库 单

№ 06364518

仓库：原材料仓库　　　　制单日期：2017年4月1日

序号	名称	规格型号	单位	数量	单价（元）	金额（元）	备注
1	车轮	Φ200*Φ125/H30mm	个	3200	46.8	149760	
2	镀锌管	Φ18*Φ15/L1000mm	根	800	280.8	224640	
3	钢管	Φ18*Φ15/L1000mm	根			0	
4	数控芯片	MCX3154A	片	400	468	187200	
5	车篷	HJ72*32*40	个	400	140.4	56160	
6	豪华型童车套件	HJTB100	套	400	351	140400	
7	舒适型童车套件	HJTB200	套		234	0	
8	经济型童车套件	HJTB300	套		93.6	0	
9	纯棉坐垫	JHM500	件		257.4	0	
10	太空棉坐垫	JHM600	件	400	117	46800	
合计	拾　万　仟　佰　拾　元　角　分						

生产：萧侥　　仓储：王储　　财务：赵财　　经办：

新通教〔2017〕ARE302号北京印刷有限公司

①生产 ②仓储 ③记账

Receipt 5: Warehouse-Out Sheet

启明星童车有限公司

生产完工报告单

№ 61742812

生产线：豪华型童车生产线

制单日期：2017年4月4日

序号	产品名称	规格型号	单位	销售订单总数	生产日期	完工日期	完工总数	入库数量	备注
1	豪华型童车	QMX2017-HH16T	辆	500	4月1日	4月4日	400	400	

原材料耗用记录

序号	材料名称	规格型号	单位	领用数量	标准用量	实际用量	损耗数量	退回数量	备注
1	车轮	Φ200*Φ125/H30mı	个	3200	3200	3200			
2	镀锌管	Φ18*Φ15/L1000mı	根	800	800	800			
3	数控芯片	MCX3154A	片	400	400	400			
4	车篷	HJ72*32*40	个	400	400	400			
5	豪华型童车套件	HJTB100	套	400	400	400			
6	太空棉坐垫	JHM600	件	400	400	400			

生产：萧侥　仓储：王储　经办：

新沪教［2017］AKE201号北京印刷有限公司

①生产 ②仓库 ③车间

Receipt 6：Finished Production Report

启明星童车有限公司

入　库　单

№ 61843852

部门：仓储部

制单日期：2017年4月4日

序号	名称	规格型号	单位	入库数量	收货仓库	货位	备注
1	豪华型童车	QMX2017-HH16T	辆	400	产成品仓库	C03	
2	舒适型童车	QMX2017-SS16T	辆				
3	经济型童车	QMX2017-JJ16T	辆				
4							
5							
6							
7							

生产：萧侥　仓储：王储　财务：赵财　经办：

新沪教［2017］AKE201号北京印刷有限公司

①生产 ②仓库 ③记账

Receipt 7：Warehouse-In Sheet

启明星童车有限公司

№ 60328836

客户名称：华晨童车商贸有限公司

销售派车单

销售派车单编号：6782337

订单编号：110201704010010

制单日期：2017 年 4 月 4 日

启运城市	北京市	到达城市	上海		收货地址	上海市包山区上大路99号	
运输方式	汽运	承 运 商	顺达物流有限公司		联系方式	18765663499	
收货负责人	李安安	联系电话	18765656785		运费账期	三个月	
货物品名	规格	单位	数量	运费单价	运输距离（公里）	运费（元）	
豪华型童车	QMX2017-HH16T	辆	500	0.09	1269	57105	
金额合计	大写	人民币 伍万柒仟壹佰零伍元整		小写	57105		

销售：罗雲　仓储：王储　财务：赵财　经办：

①客户 ②销售 ③仓储

Receipt 8: Sales Trucking Order

启明星童车有限公司

№ 60328822

客户名称：华晨童车商贸有限公司

销售发货单

销售发货单编号：8897565

订单编号：110201704010010

制单日期：2017 年 4 月 4 日

发货仓库	产成品仓库		发货时间	2017 年 4 月 4 日			
发运方式	汽运		收货地点	上海市包山区上大路99号华晨童车商贸有限公司			
承 运 商	顺达物流有限公司		联系方式	18765656785		联系人	李安安
货物品名	规格	单位	数量	含税单价	税率	金额	备注
豪华型童车	QMX2017-HH16T	辆	500	3680	0.17	1840000	
金额合计	大写	人民币 壹佰捌拾肆万元整		小写	1840000		

销售：罗雲　仓储：王储　财务：赵财　经办：

①客户 ②销售 ③仓储

Receipt 9: Sales Ship Order

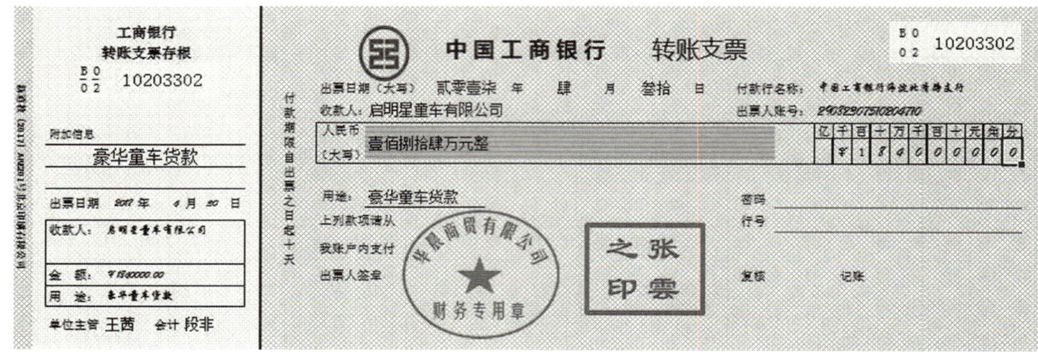

工商银行
转账支票存根
B 0
0 2 10203302
附加信息
豪华童车货款
出票日期 2017 年 4 月 20 日
收款人：启明星童车有限公司
金 额：￥1840000.00
用 途：豪华童车货款
单位主管 王茜 会计 段非

中国工商银行 转账支票
B 0
0 2 10203302
出票日期（大写） 贰零壹柒 年 肆 月 叁拾 日 付款行名称：
收款人：启明星童车有限公司 出票人账号：
人民币（大写） 壹佰捌拾肆万元整 ￥1840000000
付款期限自出票之日起十天
用途：豪华童车货款 密码
上列款项请从 行号
我账户内支付
出票人签章 复核 记账

Receipt 10: Transfer Check

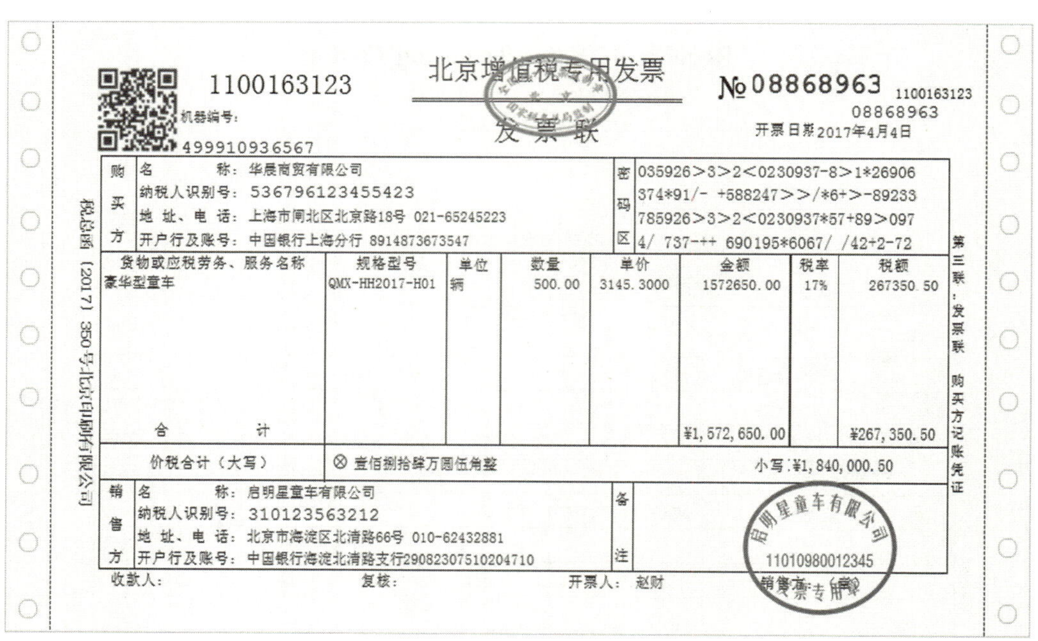

1100163123 北京增值税专用发票 №08868963 1100163123
08868963
机器编号：
499910936567 发票联 开票日期2017年4月4日

购买方	名 称：华晨商贸有限公司 纳税人识别号：536796123455423 地 址、电 话：上海市闸北区北京路18号 021-65245223 开户行及账号：中国银行上海分行 8914873673547	密码区	035926>3>2<0230937-8>1*26906 374*91/- +588247>>/*6+>-89233 785926>3>2<0230937*57+89>097 4/ 737-++ 690195*6067/ /42+2-72	

货物或应税劳务、服务名称	规格型号	单位	数量	单价	金额	税率	税额
豪华型童车	QMX-HH2017-H01	辆	500.00	3145.3000	1572650.00	17%	267350.50
合 计					¥1,572,650.00		¥267,350.50
价税合计（大写）	⊗ 壹佰捌拾肆万圆伍角整				小写：¥1,840,000.50		

销售方	名 称：启明星童车有限公司 纳税人识别号：310123563212 地 址、电 话：北京市海淀区北清路66号 010-62432881 开户行及账号：中国银行海淀北清路支行29082307510204710	备注	11010980012345

收款人： 复核： 开票人：赵财 销售方：（章）

第三联：发票联 购买方记账凭证

税总函〔2017〕350号北京印刷有限公司

Receipt 11: Value-Added Tax Invoice

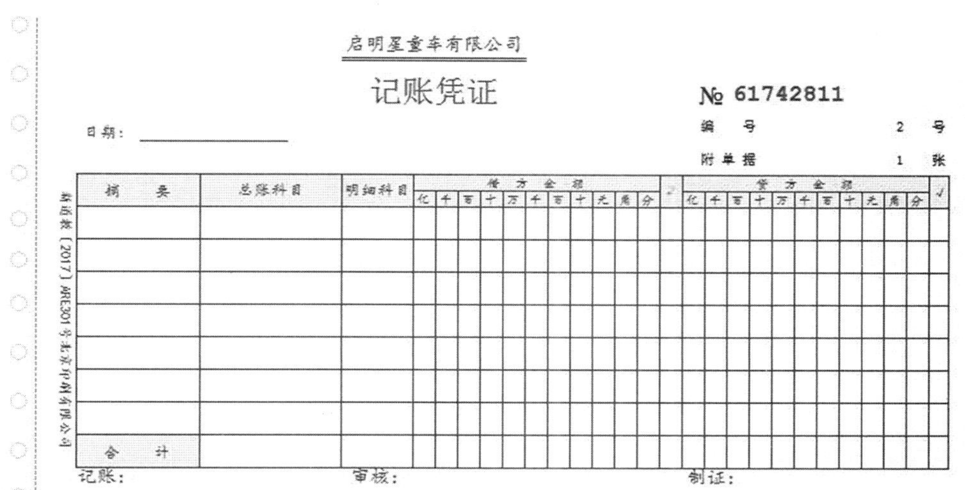

启明星童车有限公司

记账凭证

№ 61742811

日期：______

编 号 2 号

附单据 1 张

摘要	总账科目	明细科目	借方金额												贷方金额											✓
			亿	千	百	十	万	千	百	十	元	角	分		亿	千	百	十	万	千	百	十	元	角	分	
合计																										

记账： 审核： 制证：

Receipt 12: Accounting Voucher

销售收入及回款预算表

编制部门	销售部				预算期间：2017－3－31								金额单位：元
品名及规格	销售收入						销售回款						预计本月应收余款
	单位	本月订货数量	单价	订单金额	预计销量	本月预计收入	上月应收余额	前期回款	当期回款	上旬	中旬	下旬	全月合计	
豪华型童车	辆													
舒适型童车	辆													
经济型童车	辆													
合计	辆													

审批意见：同意　　签字：销售经理　　2017 年 3 月 31 日

Receipt 13: Sales Revenue and Return Budget Statement

4 月份资金支出计划表

制表部门：采购部　　金额单位：元

序号	本月资金支出计划						资金审批执行情况			备注
	单位名称	支出项目	上月账面欠款	付款比例	付款金额	付款方式	批款金额	结算方式	执行情况	
1	艾尔金属制品有限责任公司	原材料								
2	邦尼坐垫有限公司	原材料								
3	恒通车轮有限公司	原材料								
4	语阳布艺零件加工厂	原材料								
5	科尔数控科技有限公司	原材料								
6	思远布艺加工厂	原材料								
	合计									

审批意见：同意　　签字：财务经理　　2017 年 3 月 31 日

Receipt 14: Capital Expenditure Plan 1 in April

4 月份资金支出计划表

制表部门：财务部　　　　金额单位：元

序号	本月资金支出计划						资金审批执行情况			备注
	单位名称	支出项目	上月账面欠款	付款比例	付款金额	付款方式	批款金额	结算方式	执行情况	
1	财务部	工资福利								
2	财务部	个人所得税								
3	财务部	五险一金								
4	财务部	所得税								
5										
6										
	合计									

审批意见：同意　　　　签字：财务经理　　　　2017 年 3 月 31 日

Receipt 15：Capital Expenditure Plan 2 in April

4 月份资金收支平衡表

编制部门：财务部　　　　金额单位：元

收入项目	上月	本月	支出项目	上月	本月
	实际完成	计划数		实际完成	计划数
产品销售收入（现款）			材料采购支出（现款）		
其他销售收入			外部加工支出		
营业外收入			薪资支出		
收回应收款			管理费支出		
其他收入			营业外支出		
			上缴所得税		
			提取折旧基金		
			提取大修理基金		
			提取职工福利基金		
			偿还应付款		
			归还银行借款		
收入合计			支出合计		
月初结存现金和存款			月末结存现金和存款		
总计			总计		

Receipt 16：Balance of Payment April

销售计划表

产品名称	计划全年销量	1 季度计划销量	1 季度实际销量	1 季度完成率	4 月计划销售量	4 月实际销售量	4 月完成率
经济型童车							
舒适型童车							
豪华型童车							
合计							

Receipt 17：Sales Planning

4 月份物料需求计划表

编制部门：财务部　　　　编制时间：2017 年 3 月 31 日

序号	物料名称	规格型号	单位	安全库存	现存量	生产订单需求用量			需用量合计	需求日期	备注
						豪华型童车	舒适型童车	经济型童车			
1	车轮	HJΦWX125/ΦIN60(mm)	个	15,000	15,000					2017.04.01	
2	镀锌管	ΦEX16/ΦIN11/L5000(mm)	跟	3,000	3,000					2017.04.01	
3	钢管	ΦEX16/ΦIN11/L5000(mm)	跟	2,400	2,400					2017.04.01	
4	数控芯片	MCX3154A	片	600	600					2017.04.01	
5	车篷	HJ72 * 32 * 40	个	2,700	2,700					2017.04.01	
6	豪华型童车配件	HJTB300	套	600	600					2017.04.01	
7	舒适型童车配件	HJTB200	套	900	900					2017.04.01	
8	经济型童车配件	HJTB100	套	1,200	1,200					2017.04.01	
9	纯棉坐垫	HJM500	件	2,100	2,100					2017.04.01	
10	太空棉坐垫	HJM600	件	600	600					2017.04.01	

审批意见:同意　　　　签字:生产经理　　　　2017 年 3 月 31 日

Receipt 18: Material Demand Plan 1 in April

4 月份物料需求计划表

编制部门:财务部　　　　编制时间:2017 年 3 月 31 日

序号	物料名称	规格型号	单位	安全库存	现存量	生产订单需求用量			需用量合计	需求日期	备注
						豪华型童车	舒适型童车	经济型童车			
1	车轮	HJΦWX125/ΦIN60(mm)	个	15,000	15,000					2017.04.07	
2	镀锌管	ΦEX16/ΦIN11/L5000(mm)	跟	3,000	3,000					2017.04.07	
3	钢管	ΦEX16/ΦIN11/L5000(mm)	跟	2,400	2,400					2017.04.07	
4	数控芯片	MCX3154A	片	600	600					2017.04.07	
5	车篷	HJ72 * 32 * 40	个	2,700	2,700					2017.04.07	
6	豪华型童车配件	HJTB300	套	600	600					2017.04.07	
7	舒适型童车配件	HJTB200	套	900	900					2017.04.07	
8	经济型童车配件	HJTB100	套	1,200	1,200					2017.04.07	
9	纯棉坐垫	HJM500	件	2,100	2,100					2017.04.07	
10	太空棉坐垫	HJM600	件	600	600					2017.04.07	

审批意见:同意　　　　签字:生产经理　　　　2017 年 3 月 31 日

Receipt 19: Material Demand Plan 2 in April

资金支付申请表

支付项目	收款单位	付款时间	付款方式	总金额	已付金额	剩余金额	付款金额
采购支付	恒通车轮有限公司	2017.04.26					
采购支付	艾尔金属制品有限责任公司	2017.04.26					
采购支付	科尔数控科技有限公司	2017.04.26					
采购支付	思远布艺加工厂	2017.04.26					
采购支付	语阳布艺零件加工厂	2017.04.26					
采购支付	邦尼坐垫有限公司	2017.04.26					
采购支付	新耀数控科技有限公司	2017.04.26					
采购支付	京东商贸城	2017.04.26					
采购支付	顺达物流有限公司	2017.04.26					
支付上月工资	员工	2017.04.26					
代缴上月个人所得税	税务局	2017.04.26					
支付上月五险一金	税务局	2017.04.26					
支付企业所得税	税务局	2017.04.26					
申请人	财务经理	申请时间	2017.04.26	审核人	总经理	审核时间	2017.04.26

Receipt 20: Capital Payment Request Sheet

盘点单

账面日期:2017.04.30　　盘点日期:2017.04.30　　仓库:

编号	存货名称	规格型号	计量单位	账面数量	盘点数量	盈亏数量
1						
2						
3						

盘点人:仓库经理

Receipt 21: Inventory List

Subtask Four: Do you have anything to talk about the sheets above? What are the differences between your country's bills and Chinese bills?

Think Out of the Box

Table 9: Characteristics of a Great Company

✣ The company selects target markets in which it enjoys superior advantages and exits or avoids markets where it is intrinsically week.
✣ Virtually all the company's employees and departments are customer– and market–minded.
✣ There is a good working relationship between marketing, R&D, and manufacturing departments.
✣ There is a good working relationship between marketing, sales, and customer service departments.
✣ The company has designed incentive system to lead to the right behaviors.
✣ The company continuously builds and tracks customer satisfaction and loyalty.
✣ The company manages a value delivery system in partnership with strong suppliers and distributors.
✣ The company is skilled in building its brand name(s) and image.
✣ The company is flexible in meeting customers' varying requirements.

According to Table 9, can you talk about your thoughts?

Task Two: Collaborative Purchasing

Main Content

1. Understanding the collaborative purchasing
2. Understanding how to match the receipts and the steps on the screen
3. Practicing to make connection with the collaborative purchasing

Knowledge Points

1. The meaningful of collaborative purchasing
2. The meaningful of receipts on the screen
3. The meaningful of position' s receipts
4. Preliminary understanding the basic Chinese purchasing receipts

◇ Target of the task

1. Learning basic information of collaborative purchasing
2. Preliminarily understanding the Chinese collaborative purchasing receipts

4.2.1 Understanding Collaborative Purchasing

√ Please take all the orders one by one in order to understand the business receipts.

A. Supplementary products

B. Checking the quantity of products and putting them into the warehouse

C. Financial settlement

D. Purchasing order

E. Production planning

F. Purchasing planning

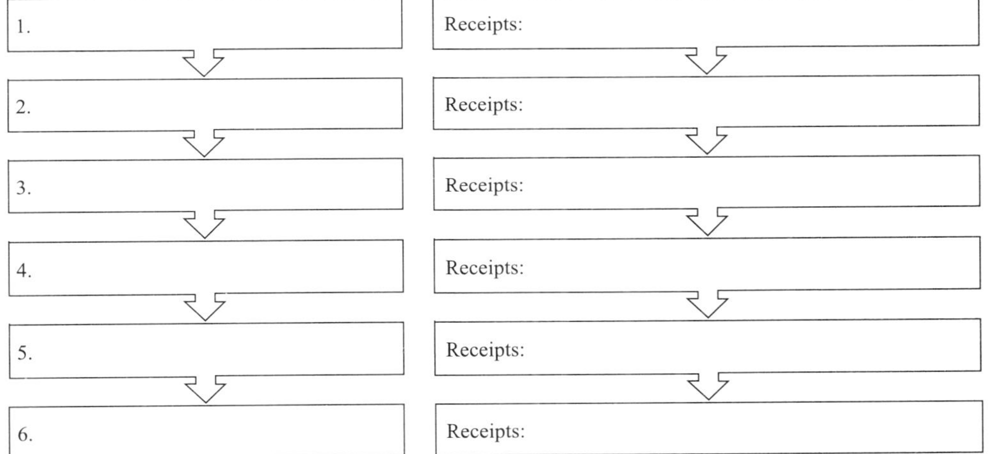

4.2.2 Real Situation Matching with Business Receipts

Subtask Five: Please write down the names of receipts on the sticky note, then put the sticky note on the cognition screen.

√ Example: write down the "Warehouse-In Sheet" on the raw material area.

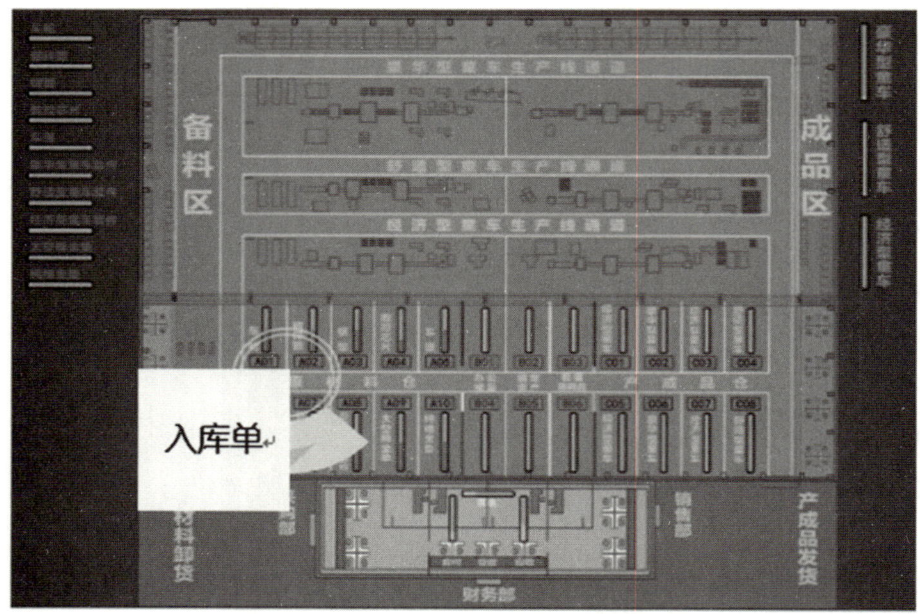

4.2.3 Practicing Collaborative Purchasing

Subtask Six: According to the screen of collaborative purchasing in ARE, please write down main assignments about the receipt on the table.

Step name	Receipt	Position	Notes
Sales order	Sales order sheet	Sales Manager	Customer name, drawer name, quantity, deadline

4.2.4 Preliminary Understanding of Basic Chinese Purchasing Receipts (Sample Only)

启明星童车有限公司

№ 65465199

4 月采购计划表

部门：采购部　　　　制表日期：2017年4月1日

序号	名称	规格型号	单位	安全库存	现存量	生产需用量	计划采购量	计划到货日期	计划到货日期	采购单价估价	采购总价估价	备注
1	车轮	Φ200*Φ125/H30mm	个	4000	4000	6400	2400					
2	镀锌管	Φ18*Φ15/L1000mm	根	1000	1000	1600	600					
3	钢管	Φ18*Φ15/L1000mm	根	2000	2000							
4	数控芯片	MCX3154A	片	500	500	800	300					
5	车篷	HJ72*32*40	个	1500	1500	800						
6	豪华型童车套件	HJTB100	套	500	500	800	300					
7	舒适型童车套件	HJTB200	套	500	500							
8	经济型童车套件	HJTB300	套	500	500							
9	纯棉坐垫	JHM500	件	1000	1000							
10	太空棉坐垫	JHM600	件	500	500	800	300					
批示意见												

制表：　　　　采购：李响

Receipt 1: Purchasing Planning Sheet

启明星童车有限公司

№ 61728893

采购订单

供应商名称：恒通车轮有限公司　　采购订单编号：CG0021

采购类型：普通采购　　制单日期：2017年4月1日

序号	品名	到货时间	单位	数量	单价	金额	备注
1	车轮	4月6日	个	2400	46.8	112320	
2							
3							
4							
5							
金额合计	大写	人民币　拾壹万贰仟叁佰贰拾元整		小写		112320	

采购：李响　　仓储：王储　　经办：

①供应商 ②采购 ③存根

Receipt 2: Purchasing Order

启明星童车有限公司

№ 61728660

供应商名称：恒通车轮有限公司

质量检验单

检验单编号：ZJ0021　　　制单日期：2017年4月6日

序号	品名	到货数量	品质要求	合格数量	不合格数量	入库数量	备注
1	车轮	2400	达标	2400	0	2400	
2							
3							
4							
5							

采购：李响　　仓储：王储　　检验：郑浩

新通数〔2017〕ARE201号北京印刷有限公司

①供应商 ②采购 ③存根

Receipt 3: Quality Inspection List

启明星童车有限公司

№ 61742812

供货单位：恒通车轮有限公司

材料入库单

制单日期：2017年　4月　6日

序号	名称	规格型号	单位	数量	单价（元）	金额（元）	备注
1	车轮	Φ200*125/H30mm	个	2400	46.8	112320	
2							
3							
4							
5							
合计	人民币	拾壹万贰仟叁佰贰拾元整					

会计：赵财　　李响　　仓储：王储　　经办：

新通数〔2017〕ARE301号北京印刷有限公司

①存根 ②仓库 ③采购

Receipt 4: Material Warehouse-In Sheet

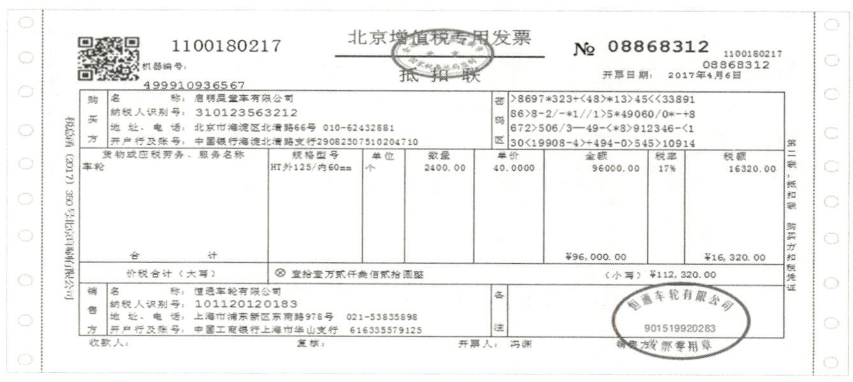

1100180217　　北京增值税专用发票　　№ 08868312

抵扣联

机器编号：499910936567

1100180217
08868312
开票日期：2017年4月6日

购买方
名　　称：启明星童车有限公司
纳税人识别号：310123563212
地 址、电 话：北京市海淀区北清路66号 010-62432881
开户行及账号：中国银行海淀北清路支行2908230751020471O

密码区
>8697*323+<48>*13>45<<33891
86>8-2/-*1//1>5*49060/0*-+8
672>506/3—49-<*8>912346-<1
30<19908-4>+494-0>545>10914

货物或应税劳务、服务名称	规格型号	单位	数量	单价	金额	税率	税额
车轮	HT外125/内60mm	个	2400.00	40.0000	96000.00	17%	16320.00
合　计					¥96,000.00		¥16,320.00
价税合计（大写）	⊗壹拾壹万贰仟叁佰贰拾圆整				（小写）¥112,320.00		

销售方
名　　称：恒通车轮有限公司
纳税人识别号：101120120183
地 址、电 话：上海市浦东新区东南路978号 021-53835898
开户行及账号：中国工商银行上海市华山支行 616335579125

备注：恒通车轮有限公司 901519920283 发票专用章

收款人：　　复核：　　开票人：冯渊　　销售方：（章）

税总函〔2017〕350号北京印刷有限公司

第二联：抵扣联　购买方扣税凭证

Receipt 5: Value-Added Tax Invoice (Deduction form)

1100180217　　北京增值税专用发票　　№ 08868312　　1100180217 08868312

机器编号：499910936567　　发票联　　开票日期：2017年4月6日

购买方	名称：启明星童车有限公司 纳税人识别号：310123563212 地址、电话：北京市海淀区北清路66号 010-62432881 开户行及账号：中国银行海淀北清路支行290823075102O4710	密码区	>8697*323+<48>*13>45<<33891 86>8-2/-*1//1>5*49060/0*--8 672>506/3—49-<8>912346-<1 30<19908-4>+49<-0>545>10914

货物或应税劳务、服务名称	规格型号	单位	数量	单价	金额	税率	税额
车轮	HT外125/内60mm	个	2400.00	40.0000	96000.00	17%	16320.00
合计					¥96,000.00		¥16,320.00
价税合计（大写）	⊗壹拾壹万贰仟叁佰贰拾圆整				（小写）¥112,320.00		

销售方	名称：恒通车轮有限公司 纳税人识别号：101120120183 地址、电话：上海市浦东新区东南路978号 021-53835898 开户行及账号：中国工商银行上海市华山支行 616335579125	备注	恒通车轮有限公司 901519920283 销售方（章）

收款人：　　复核：　　开票人：冯渊　　销售方：（章）

第三联：发票联　购买方记账凭证

Receipt 6: Value-Added Tax Invoice (Invoice form)

启明星童车有限公司

领　料　单

部门：生产部　　№ 65465199　　制单日期：2017年4月6日

序号	名称	规格型号	单位	申领数量	实发数量	退库数量	备注
1	车轮	Φ200*125/H30mm	个	2400	2400		
2	镀锌管	Φ18*15/L1000mm	根	600	600		
3	钢管	Φ18*15/L1000mm	根				
4	数控芯片	MCX3154A	片	300	300		
5	车篷	HJ72*32*40	个	300	300		
6	豪华型童车套件	HJTB100	套	300	300		
7	舒适型童车套件	HJTB200	套				
8	经济型童车套件	HJTB300	套				
9	纯棉坐垫	JHM500	件				
10	太空棉坐垫	JHM600	件	300	300		
用途	按订单生产						

生产：萧侥　　记账：赵财　　仓储：王储　　经办：

①存根 ②仓库 ③记账

Receipt 7: Picking List

启明星童车有限公司

材料出库单

仓库：原材料仓库　　№ 06364518　　制单日期：2017年4月6日

序号	名称	规格型号	单位	数量	单价（元）	金额（元）	备注
1	车轮	Φ200*125/H30mm	个	2400			
2	镀锌管	Φ18*15/L1000mm	根	600			
3	钢管	Φ18*15/L1000mm	根				
4	数控芯片	MCX3154A	片	300			
5	车篷	HJ72*32*40	个	300			
6	豪华型童车套件	HJTB100	套	300			
7	舒适型童车套件	HJTB200	套				
8	经济型童车套件	HJTB300	套				
9	纯棉坐垫	JHM500	件				
10	太空棉坐垫	JHM600	件	300			
合计	拾　万　仟　佰　拾　元　角　分						

会计：赵财　　记账：　　仓储：王储　　经办：

①存根 ②仓库 ③记账

Receipt 8: Material Warehouse-Out List

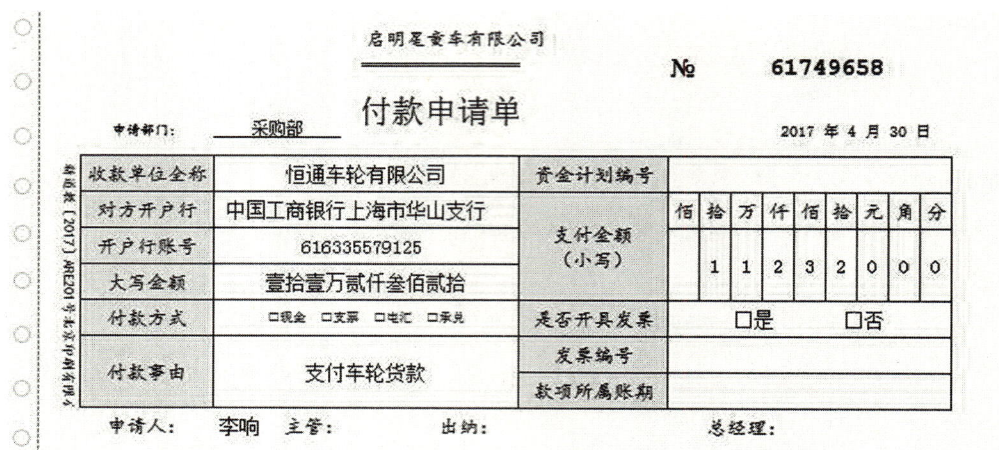

启明星童车有限公司

№ 61749658

付款申请单

申请部门：采购部　　　　2017 年 4 月 30 日

收款单位全称	恒通车轮有限公司	资金计划编号									
对方开户行	中国工商银行上海市华山支行	支付金额（小写）	佰	拾	万	仟	佰	拾	元	角	分
开户行账号	616335579125			1	1	2	3	2	0	0	0
大写金额	壹拾壹万贰仟叁佰贰拾										
付款方式	□现金　□支票　□电汇　□承兑	是否开具发票	□是　□否								
付款事由	支付车轮货款	发票编号									
		款项所属账期									

申请人：李响　主管：　　出纳：　　总经理：

Receipt 9: Payment Application Form

Subtask Seven: Do you have anything to talk about the sheets above, What are the differences between your country's bills and Chinese bills?

Think Out of the Box

Table 10: Company's Metrics

<table>
<tr>
<td>Sales Metrics
✓ Sales growth
✓ Market share
✓ Sales from new products</td>
<td>Distribution Metrics
✓ Number of outlets
✓ Weighted distribution
✓ Distribution gains
✓ Average stock volume
✓ Storage time
✓ Out of stock frequency
✓ Share of shelves
✓ Average point-to-point sales revenue</td>
</tr>
<tr>
<td>Customer Readiness to Buy Metrics
✓ Awareness
✓ Preference
✓ Purchase intention
✓ Trial rate
✓ Repurchase rate</td>
<td rowspan="2">Customer metrics
✓ Customer complaints
✓ Customer satisfaction
✓ Ratio of promoters to detractors
✓ Customer acquisition costs
✓ New-customer gains
✓ Customer losses
✓ Customer loyalty
✓ Retention rate
✓ Customer lifetime value
✓ Customer equity
✓ Customer profitability
✓ Return on customer</td>
</tr>
<tr>
<td>Communication Metrics
✓ Spontaneous brand awareness
✓ Top brand awareness
✓ Prompted brand awareness
✓ Spontaneous advertising awareness
✓ Prompted advertising awareness
✓ Effective reach
✓ Effective frequency
✓ Gross rating points
✓ Response rate</td>
</tr>
</table>

According to Table 10, can you talk about your thoughts?

Expansion of Mind

Table 11: Profiles of Major Media Types

Medium	Advantages	Limitations
Newspaper	Flexibility; timeliness; good local market coverage; broad acceptance; high believability	Short life; poor reproduction quality; small "pass-along" audience
Television	Combining sight, sound, and motion; appealing to the senses; high attention; high reach	High absolute cost; high clutter; fleeting exposure; less audience selectivity
Direct mail	Audience selectivity; flexibility; no ad competition within the same medium; personalization	Relatively high cost; "junk mail" image
Radio	Mass use; high geographic and demographic selectivity; low cost	Audio presentation only; lower attention than television; non-standardized rate structure; fleeting exposure

Continued

Medium	Advantages	Limitations
Magazine	High geographic and demographic selectivity; credibility and prestige; high-quality reproduction; long life; good pass-along readership	Long ad purchase lead time; some waste in circulation
Outdoor advertising	Flexibility; highly repeated exposure; low cost; low competition	Limited audience selectivity; limited creativity
Yellow page	Excellent local coverage; high believability; wide reach; low cost	High competition; long ad purchase lead time; limited creativity
Newsletter	Very high selectivity; full control; interactive opportunities; relatively low cost	Waste of cost
Brochure	Flexibility; full control; attractive messages	Overproduction can lead to runaway costs
Telephone	Many users; opportunity to give a personal touch	Relatively high cost; increasing consumer resistance
Internet	High selectivity; interactive possibilities; relatively low cost	Increasing clutter

Chapter Five

Evaluation

Task One: General Manager Meeting

Main Content

1. How to check the meeting timetable
2. How to summarize the company's operation
3. How to record the meeting content

Knowledge Points

1. Organizing meetings by General Manager
2. The conclusion by General Manager
3. General Manager meeting's content

◇ Target of the task

1. Learning to organize meetings
2. Learning to summarize the company's operation
3. Training how to record the meeting content

5.1.1 Checking the Schedule of Meeting

√ According to the schedule of the course to organize the meeting.

1. The main points of monthly meeting content:

____

____

2. General Manager's responsibility to the employees:

____

____

3. General Manager's work with the employees:

____

____

4. The problems in the work:

____

____

5. Working experience:

____

____

5.1.2 General Manager Report

√ General Manager have a report in the meeting.

The main points in General Manager's report:

1. The overall operation of the company.
2. The overall management of the company.
3. Management experience of General Manager.
4. The important things in the management work.
5. The disadvantages of the management work.

5.1.3 Meeting Content

✓ Record meeting process and make a decision for the company strategy.

Meeting time:
Place:
Participants:
Host:
Main points:

According to the General Manager meeting, do you have any other ideas that you think General Manager should know?

____

____

____

____

____

____

____

____

____

Task Two: Analytical Thinking

Main Content

1. How to analyze sales management
2. How to analyze purchasing management
3. How to analyze storage management
4. How to analyze production management
5. How to analyze financial management

Knowledge

1. The overall operation of the company

◇ Target of the task

Learning the overall operation of the company

5.2.1 Sales Management

✓ Please think about the position of Sales Manager and the flow of sales, and then answer the questions below.

1. What is the meaning of sales-production-procurement collaboration? What kind of information do they have to share with other departments? Why?

2. What is the most important thing after receiving sales order?

3. Why is sales delivery the most critical step in sales management?

Think: Which one should be the first, sales order or sales delivery?

5.2.2 Purchasing Management

✓ Please think about the position of Purchasing Manager and the flow of purchasing, and then answer the questions below.

1. What is the meaning of sales-production-storage-procurement collaboration? What kind of information do they have to share with other departments? Why?

2. Should raw material warehouse-in sheet accord with purchasing order, the

quantity of arrived product or quality inspection list?

3. Should raw material warehouse-in sheet put all raw materials together? Why?

5.2.3 Warehousing Management

✓ Please think about the position of warehousing and the flow of warehousing, and then answer the questions below.

1. If there are products in the storage, what kind of production planning and purchasing planning do we need to do?

2. What is the difference between paper work and system information during the process of production picking and warehouse-out?

3. If the actual quantity of warehouse-out is not the same with that of picking list, how to deal with it?

5.2.4 Production Management

✓Please think about the position of Production Manager and the flow of production, and then answer the questions below.

1. Why do we have to check the raw materials?

2. If there are disqualified raw materials in the production process, how to deal with it?

3. How to check the product's quality ?

4. Should we check the quality of the finished product? Who should do it? How to design the system?

5.2.5 Financial Management

✓Please think about the position of Financial Manager and the flow of finance, and then answer the questions below.

1. Why do we have to analyze capital planning sheet?

2. After discussing with Financial Manager, should CEO have a report to the lecturer?

3. What is the meaning of the inventory reconciliation at the end of the month?

Task Three: Evaluation

Main content

1. Evaluating yourself
2. Evaluating each other
3. Evaluating General Manager

Knowledge Points

The overall ARE

◇ Target of the task

1. Learning the overall ARE

5.3.1 Evaluating Yourself

√ Please finish all the questions below after course, and then compare with the questionnaire that we have finished in the first class.

According to your feeling, finish the questions in the questionnaire. (5=Satisfactory, 4=Relatively satisfactory, 3=Acceptable, 2=Dissatisfactory, 1=Quite dissatisfactory)												
No.	Program	Content	Before the lessons					After the lessons				
			5	4	3	2	1	5	4	3	2	1
1	Structure of enterprises	Can you image the overall structure of enterprises?										
2	Business processes	Can you fully understand the logistics flow, capital flow, and information flow in the enterprise?										
3	Knowledge perception	Can you build a team with 4-6 team members, and organize them well?										
4	Position understanding	Can you fully understand the responsibility of the position?										
5	Management planning	Can you fully understand the importance of making schedule?										
6	Receipts and reports	Can you fully understand the meaning of the receipts and reports?										
7	Cooperative capability	Can you fully understand the importance of the cooperation between different departments?										
8	Communication capability	Do you know the importance to communicate with other departments?										
9	Operation	In the management process, can you find the problems of operation?										

Continued

According to your feeling, finish the questions in the questionnaire. (5=Satisfactory, 4=Relatively satisfactory, 3=Acceptable, 2=Dissatisfactory, 1=Quite dissatisfactory)												
No.	Program	Content	Before the lessons					After the lessons				
			5	4	3	2	1	5	4	3	2	1
10	Logic	If you were the boss, could you take into consideration all of the business processes such as employment, capital, supplier and sales.										

5.3.2 Evaluating Each Other

✓According to the team members' working performance, give the points to each other.

Name	Position	Grade	Notes

5.3.3 General Manager Evaluation

✓According to the team members' working performance, General Manager gives the points to each other.

Name	Position	Grade	Notes
	Sales Manager		
	Purchasing Manager		
	Production Manager		
	Storage Manager		
	Financial Manager		

5.3.4 Composite Results

Name	Position	Self-evaluation	Mutual-evaluation	Teacher's noted
	Sales Manager			
	Purchasing Manager			
	Production Manager			
	Storage Manager			
	Financial Manager			

Think Out of the Box

Table 12: Major Consumer Promotion Tools

1. Consumers are more likely to choose an alternative (a household bread maker) after a relatively inferior option (a slightly better, but significantly more expensive household bread maker) is added to the choice set.
2. Consumers are more likely to choose an alternative that appears to be a compromise in the particular choice set under consideration, even if it is not the best alternative in any one dimension.
3. The choices consumers make influence their assessment of their own tastes and preferences.
4. Making people focus their more attention on one of the two considered alternatives tends to enhance the perceived attractiveness and choice probability of that alternative.
5. The way consumers compare products that vary in price and perceived quality (by features or brand name) and the way those products are displayed in the store (by brand or model type) both affect their willingness to pay more for additional features or a better-known brand.

Continued

6. Consumers who think about the possibility that their purchase decisions will turn out to be wrong are more likely to choose better-known brands.
7. Consumers with possible feelings of regret about missing an opportunity are more likely to choose a product currently on sale rather than to wait for a better selling price or buy a higher-priced item.
8. Consumers' choices are often influenced by subtle (and theoretically inconsequential) changes in the way alternatives are described.
9. Consumers who make purchases for later consumption appear to make systematic errors in predicting their future preferences.
10. Consumers' predictions of their future tastes are not accurate–they do not really know how they will feel after consuming the same flavor of yogurt or ice cream several times.
11. Consumers often overestimate the duration of their overall emotional reactions to future events (moves, financial windfalls, outcomes of sporting events).
12. Consumers often overestimate their future consumption, especially if there is limited availability (which may explain why Black Jack and other gums have higher sales when availability is limited to several months per year than when they are offered year round).
13. In anticipating future consumption opportunities, consumers often assume they will want or need more variety than they actually do.
14. Consumers are less likely to choose alternatives with product features or promotional premiums that have little or no value, even when these features and premiums are optional (like the opportunity to purchase a collector's plate) and do not reduce the actual value of the product in any way.
15. Consumers are less likely to choose products selected by others for reasons they find irrelevant, even when these other reasons do not suggest anything positive or negative about the product's values.
16. Consumers' interpretations and evaluations of past experiences are greatly influenced by the ending and trend of events. A positive event at the end of a service experience can color later reflections and evaluations of the experience as a whole.

According to the major consumer promotion tools, write your thoughts:

____

____

____

Expansion of Mind

The Marketing Research Process

Step 1: Define the problem, the decision alternatives, and the research objectives

Step 2: Develop the research plan

√ Data sources

√ Research approaches

√ Survey research

√ Behavioral research

√ Experimental research

√ Research instruments

√ Sampling plan

√ Number of local vehicles

Step 3: Collect the information

Step 4: Analyze the information

Step 5: Present the findings

Step 6: Make the decision

According to the marketing research process, write your ideas:

Flow Chart: Sales Force Objective and Strategy

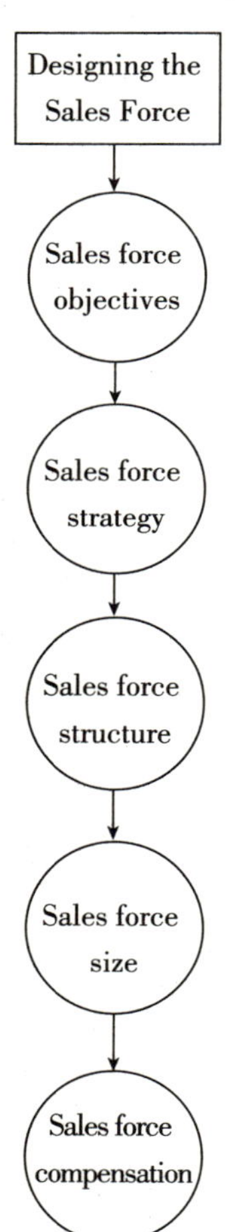

Companies need to define specific sales force objectives. For example, a company might want its sales representatives to spend 80 percent of their time with current customers and 20 percent with prospects, and 85 percent of their time on established products and 15 percent on new products. Regardless of the selling context, salesmen perform one or more specific tasks:

Prospecting. Searching for prospects or leads.

Targeting. Deciding how to allocate their time between prospects and customers.

Communication. Communicating information about the company's products and services.

Selling. Approaching, presenting, answering questions, achieving objective, and closing sales.

Servicing. Providing various services to the customers —consulting on problems, rendering technical assistance, arranging financing, expediting delivery.

Information gathering. Conducting market research and doing intelligence work.

Allocation. Deciding which customers will get scarce products during product shortages.

According to the sales force objective and strategy, write your ideas.

Table 13: Types of Questions

Name	Description	Example
A. Closed-End Questions		
Dichotomous question	A question with two possible answers	When arranging this trip, did you personally phone American? ☐ Yes ☐ No
Multiple question	A question with three or more answers	With whom are you traveling on this flight? ☐ No one ☐ One child ☐ Spouse ☐ Business associates/friends/relatives ☐ Spouse and children ☐ An organized tour group

Continued

Name	Description	Example
Likert scale question	A statement with which the respondent shows their attitudes	Small airlines generally give better service than large ones. ☐ Strongly disagree ☐ Disagree ☐ Neither agree nor disagree ☐ Agree ☐ Strongly agree
Semantic differe-ntial question	A scale connecting two bipolar words. The respondent selects the point that represents his or her opinion	American Airlines Large ______________ Small Experienced __________ Inexperienced Modern ___________ Old-fashioned
Importance scale question	A scale that rates the impor-tance of some attribute	Airline in-flight service to me is ☐ Extremely important ☐ Very important ☐ Somewhat important ☐ Not very important ☐ Not at all important
Rating scale question	A scale that rates some attri-bute from "poor" to "excellent"	American in-flight service is ☐ Excellent ☐ Very good ☐ Good ☐ Fair ☐ Poor
Intention-to-buy-scale question	A scale that describes the respondent's intention to buy	If an in-flight telephone was available on a long flight, I would ☐ Definitely buy ☐ Probably buy ☐ Not be sure to buy ☐ Probably not buy ☐ Definitely not buy

Continued

Name	Description	Example
B. Open-End Questions		
Completely unstructured question	A question that respondents can answer in an almost unlimited number of ways	What is your opinion of American Airlines?
Word association question	Words are presented, one at a time, and respondents mention the first word that comes to mind	What is the first word that comes to your mind when you hear the following words? Airline __________ American __________ Travel __________
Sentence completion question	An incomplete sentence is presented and respondents need to complete the sentence	When I choose an airline, the most important consideration in my decision is__________
Story completion question	An incomplete story is presented, and respondents are asked to complete it	"I flew to America a few days ago. I noticed that the exterior and interior of the plane had very bright colors. This aroused in me the following thoughts and feelings..." Now complete the story.
Picture question	A picture of two characters is presented, with one making a statement. Respondents are asked to identify the two characters and fill in the empty balloon	
Thematic Apperception Test (TAT) question	A picture is presented and respondents are asked to make up a story about what they think is happening or may happen in the picture	

Appendix 1 Initial Data in April

Table 1: Initial Asset Balance

Capital Balance Sheet			
Date:			
Asset		**Liability and right**	
Program	**Initial (yuan)**	**Program**	**Initial (yuan)**
Cash	11,597.00	Accounts payable	12,116,520.00
Bank statement	22,810,164.76	Other accounts payable	274,355.10
Receivables payable	20,712,000.00	Payroll payable	377,644.72
Bad-debt provision	2,716.00	Tax payable	5,039,510.31
Inventory	3,006,223.00	Long-term loan	0.00
Among: Raw material	3,006,223.00	Total balance	17,808,030.13
Finished products (Inventory goods)	0.00	Paid-up capital	
Immobilizations	48,624,000.00		
Minus: Accumulated depreciation	4,852,839.47		63,000,000.00
Net immobilizations	43,771,160.53	Earned surplus	3,375,745.18
Intangible assets	3,000,000.00	Current year profit	7,441,003.46
Minus: Accumulated amortization	175,508.00	Distribution of profits	1,508,142.52
Net intangible assets	2,824,492.00	Total rights	75,324,891.16
Total assets	93,132,921.29	Total liability and right	93,132,921.29
Writer:		Auditor:	

Table 2: Initial Raw Material List

Name of inventory	Number	Supplier	Safety inventory (6 days)
Steel tube	2,400	EI Metal Products Co., Ltd.	2,400
Galvanized tube	3,000		3,000
Pure cotton cushion	2,100	Bonney Cushion Co., Ltd.	2,100
Space cotton cushion	600		600
Canvas top	2,700	Siyuan Cloth Art Processing Factory	2,700
Wheel	15,000	Hengtong Wheel Co., Ltd.	15,000
Digital chip	600	Keying Digital Technology Co., Ltd.	600
Economical set	1,200	Language Yang Cloth Art Kit Processing Factory	1,200
Comfort set	900		900
Luxury set	600		600
Children's parasol	100	JD.com	10
A small ball	100		10
Cushion	100		10
Total	29,400		29,130

Table 3: Initial Finished Product List

Name of inventory	Number	Amount (yuan)
Economical baby stroller	0.00	0.00
Comfort baby stroller	0.00	0.00
Luxury baby stroller	0.00	0.00
Total	0.00	0.00

Table 4: Receivable Payable

Client	Name of inventory	Number	Amount (yuan)	Total
Beijing Xinyi Trading Co., Ltd.	Economical baby stroller	1,000	1,400,000.00	4,976,000.00
	Comfort baby stroller	600	1,368,000.00	
	Luxury baby stroller	600	2,208,000.00	
Changchun Chunmeng Trade Co., Ltd.	Economical baby stroller	2,600	3,640,000.00	15,736,000.00
	Comfort baby stroller	2,400	5,472,000.00	
	Luxury baby stroller	1,800	6,624,000.00	
Total		9,000	20,712,000.00	20,712,000.00

Table 5: Account Payable

Supplier	Name of inventory	Amount (yuan)	Total
EI Metal Products Co., Ltd.	Galvanized tube	3,032,640	4,043,520
	Steel tube	1,010,880	
Bonney Cushion Co., Ltd.	Space cotton cushion	617,760	1,389,960
	Pure cotton cushion	772,200	
Hengtong Wheel Co., Ltd.	Wheel	2,414,880	2,414,880
Siyuan Cloth Art Processing Factory	Canvas top	1,263,600	1,263,600
Keying Digital Technology Co., Ltd.	Digital chip	1,123,200	1,123,200
Language Yang Cloth Art Kit Processing Factory	Economical set	336,960	1,881,360
	Comfort set	702,000	
	Luxury set	842,400	
Total			12,116,520

Table 6: Tax Payable List

Name	Amount (yuan)
Unpaid VAT	3,446,568.25
Income tax	1,592,636.88
Personal income tax payable	305.18

Table 7: Initial Inventory Purchasing Price

Name of inventory	Unit price (tax include, yuan)	Supplier
Steel tube	140.4	EI Metal Products Co., Ltd.
Galvanized tube	280.8	
Pure cotton cushion	117	Bonney Cushion Co., Ltd.
Space cotton cushion	257.4	
Canvas top	140.4	Siyuan Cloth Art Processing Factory
Wheel	46.8	Hengtong Wheel Co., Ltd.
Chip	468	Keying Digital Technology Co., Ltd.
Economical set	93.6	Language Yang Cloth Art Kit Processing Factory
Comfort set	234	
Luxury set	351	
Children's parasol	35.1	JD.com
A small ball	11.7	
Cushion	23.4	
Economical baby stroller	1,400	
Comfort baby stroller	2,280	
Luxury baby stroller	3,680	

Appendix 2 Tables of Accounting Terms in Chinese and English

Table 1: Junior Accountant Terms in Chinese and English

Junior Accountant	
Accounting terms in Chinese	Accounting terms in English
对账	Checking
对应账户	Corresponding Accounts
定期清查	Periodic Checking
定期盘存制	Periodic Inventory System
订本式账簿	Bound Book
调整账户	Adjustment Accounts
调整分录	Adjustment Journal Entry
单式记账凭证	Single Account Title Voucher
单式记账法	Single-Entry Bookkeeping
从属账户	Secondary Accounts
成本计算账户	Costing Accounts
财产清查	Physical Inventory
簿记	Bookkeeping
不定期清查	Non-Periodic Checking
补充登记法	Correction by Extre Recording
表外账户	Off-Balance Sheet Accounts
备抵账户	Provision Accounts

Continued

Junior Accountant	
备抵附加账户	Provision and Adjunct Accounts
备查账簿	Memorandum
序时账簿	Book of Chronological Entry
一次凭证	Single-Record Document
银行存款日记账	Deposit Journal
永续盘存制	Perpetual Inventory System
原始凭证	Source Document
暂记账户	Suspense Accounts
增减记账法	Increase-Decrease Bookkeeping
债券结算账户	Accounts for Settlement of Claim
债权债务结算账户	Accounts for Settlement of Claim and Debt
债务结算账户	Accounts for Settlement of Debt
账户	Account
账户编号	Account Number
账户对应关系	Debit-Credit Relationship
账项调整	Adjustment of Account
专用记账凭证	Special-Purpose Voucher
转回分录	Reversing Entry
资金来源账户	Accounts of Sources of Funds
资产负债账户	Balance Sheet Accounts
转账凭证	Transfer Voucher
资金运用账户	Accounts of Application of Funds
自制原始凭证	Internal Source Document
总分类账簿	General Ledger
总分类账户	General Account
附加账户	Adjunct Accounts
付款凭证	Payment Voucher

Continued

Junior Accountant	
分类账簿	Ledger
多栏式日记账核算方式	Bookkeeping Procedure Using Columnar Journal
结账	Closing Account
结账分录	Closing Entry
借贷记账法	Debit-Credit Bookkeeping
局部清查	Partial Check
卡片式账簿	Card Book
跨期摊提账户	Inter-Period Allocation Accounts
累计凭证	Multiple-Record Document
联合账簿	Compound Book
明细分类账簿	Subsidiary Ledger
明细分类账户	Subsidiary Account
盘点账户	Inventory Accounts
平行登记	Parallel Recording
全面清查	Complete Check
日记总账	Combined Journal and Ledger
三式记账法	Triple-Entry Bookkeeping
实账户	Real Accounts
试算表	Trial Balance
试算平衡	Trial Balancing
收付记账法	Receipts-Payment Bookkeeping
收款凭证	Receipt Voucher
损益表账户	Income Statement Accounts
通用日记账凭证	General Purpose Voucher
通用日记账核算形式	Bookkeeping Procedure Using General Journal
外来原始凭证	Source Document from Outside
现金日记账	Cash Journal

Continued

Junior Accountant	
虚账户	Nominal Accounts
汇总原始凭证	Cumulative Source Document
汇总原始凭证核算形式	Bookkeeping Procedure Using Summary Vouchers
工作底稿	Working Paper
复式记账凭证	Multiple Account Titles Voucher
复式记账法	Double Entry Bookkeeping
复合分录	Compound Entry
画线更正法	Correction by Drawing a Straight Line
汇总原始凭证	Cumulative Source Document
会计凭证	Accounting Document
会计科目表	Chart of Accounts
会计科目	Account Title
红字更正法	Correction by Using Red Ink
会计核算形式	Bookkeeping Procedures
过账	Posting
会计分录	Accounting Entry
会计循环	Accounting Cycle
会计账簿	Book of Accounts
活页式账簿	Loose-Leaf Book
集合分配账户	Clearing Accounts
计价对比账户	Matching Accounts
记账方法	Bookkeeping Methods
记账规则	Recording Rules
记账凭证	Voucher
记账凭证核算形式	Bookkeeping Proceed Reusing Vouchers
记账凭证汇总表核算形式	Bookkeeping Procedure Using Categorized Account Summary
简单分录	Simple Entry
结算账户	Settlement Accounts

Table 2: Intermediate Accountant Terms in Chinese and English

Intermediate Accountant	
Accounting terms in Chinese	Accounting terms in English
期间费用	Period Expense
收入的确认	Recognition of Revenue
公司债券发行价格	Corporate Bond Issuing Price
固定资产折旧	Depreciation of Fixed Assets
可转换债券	Convertible Bonds
加速折旧法	Accelerated Depreciation Methods
营业外收支净额	Net Non-Operating Income and Expenditure
公司债券利率	Interest Rate on Debenture
应收账款出借	Assignment of Accounts Receivable
无担保债券	Debenture Bonds
后进先出法	Last-in，First-out（LIFO）Method
其他货币资金	Other Monetary Assets
应付票据贴现	Discount on Notes Payable
先进先出法	First-in，First-out（FIFO）Method
再发建工程	Construction in Process
固定资产更换与固定资产改良	Improvements and Replacement of Fixed Assets
实地盘存制	Periodic Inventory System
收益总括观点	All-Inclusive Concept of Income
损益表法	Income Statement Approach
可变现净值法	Net Realizable Value
应付福利费	Welfare Payable
固定资产扩建	Additions of Fixed Assets
应收账款出售	Sale or Factoring of Accounts Receivable
或有负债	Contingent Liability
销货退回与折让	Sales Returns and Allowances

Continued

Intermediate Accountant	
零售价格法	Retail Method
现金折扣	Cash Discount
公司债券	Bonds Payable
销售法	Sale Method
应付票据	Notes Payable
认股权	Stock Rights
固定资产修理	Repairs and Maintenance of Fixed Assets
有担保债券	Mortgage Bonds
销售费用	Selling Expenses
应付股利	Dividends Payable
应收票据	Notes Receivable
无形资产	Intangible Assets
收款法	Collection Method
所得税	Income Tax
流动负债	Current Liabilities
生产法	Production Method
废弃和重置法	Retirement and Replacement Method
盘存法	Inventory Method
流动资产	Current Assets
购货折扣	Purchases Discounts
商誉	Goodwill
应收账款	Accounts Receivable
投资收益	Investment Income
营业利润	Operating Income
股本	Capital Stock
公司债券偿还	Redemption of Bonds
坏账	Bad Debts

Continued

Intermediate Accountant	
固定资产重估价	Revaluations of Fixed Assets
银行存款	Cash in Bank
固定资产	Fixed Assets
利润分配	Profit Distribution
应计费用	Accrued Expense
商标权	Trademark Right
净利润	Net Income
应付利润	Profit Payable
未分配利润	Undistributed Profits
收益债券	Income Bonds
货币资金	Cash and Cash Equivalents
利息资本化	Capitalization of Interests
法定公益金	Statutory Welfare Reserve
工程物资	Engineer Material
预付账款	Advance to Supplier
其他应收款	Other Receivables
现金	Cash
预收账款	Advance Received from Customers
公司债券发行	Corporate Bond Floatation
应付工资	Wages Payable
实收资本	Paid-In Capital
盈余公积	Surplus Reserves
管理费用	Management Fee
股利	Dividend
应交税费	Taxes Payable
负商誉	Negative Goodwill
费用的确定	Recognition of Expense

Continued

Intermediate Accountant	
短期投资	Temporary Investment
短期借款	Short-Term Borrowing
递延资产	Deferred Charges
低值易耗品	Low-Value Consumption Goods
当期经营观点	Current Operating Concept of Income
存货销售的影响	Effects on Inventory Errors
折旧	Depreciation
折旧方法	Depreciation Method
折旧率	Depreciation Rate
支出	Payment
直线法	Straight-line Method
专利权	Patents
住房基金	Housing Fund
重置成本法	Replacement Costing
专有技术	Know-how
专营权	Franchises
资本公积	Capital Reserves
自然资源	Natural Resources
存货	Inventory
偿债基金	Sinking Fund
长期应付款	Long-Term Payables
长期投资	Long-Term Investments
长期借款	Long-Term Loans
长期负债	Long-term Liability of Long-term Debt
财务费用	Financing Expenses
拨定留存收益	Appropriated Retained Earnings
标准成本法	Standard Costing Method

Continued

Intermediate Accountant	
变动成本法	Variable Costing
包装物	Wrap-page
版权	Copyrights

Table 3: Senior Accountant Terms in Chinese and English

Senior Accountant	
Accounting terms in Chinese	Accounting terms in English
独立董事	Independent Director
市场附加值	Market Value Added（MVA）
投资中心	Investment Center
利润中心	Profit Center
酌量性费用中心	Discretionary Expense Center
收入中心	Revenue Center
合并前利润	Pre-acquisition Income
现金分配计划	Cash Distribution Plan
安全付款表	Safe Payments Schedule
合并每股收益	Consolidated EPS
期货交易市场	Market of Futures Transaction
期货交易	Futures Transaction
举债经营融资租赁	Leveraged Lease
金融工具	Financial Instruments
企业集团	Business Group
年度报告	Annual Report
内部往来	Transactions Between Home Office and Branches
合伙企业	Partnership Enterprise

Continued

Senior Accountant	
合并资产负债表	Consolidated Balance Sheet
合并主体的所得税会计	Accounting for Income Taxes of Consolidated Entities
合并现金流量表	Consolidated Statement of Cash Flow
合并价差	Cost-Book Value Differentials
合并会计报表	Consolidated Financial Statements
购买法	Purchase Method
企业整体价值	The Value of an Enterprise as a Whole
权益结合法	Pooling of Interest Method
期内所得税分摊	Intra-period Tax Allocation
期末存货的未实现损益	Unrealized Profit in Ending Inventory
公司间的长期资产业务	Intercompany Transaction in Long-term Assets
名义货币保全	Maintaining Capital in Units of Money
基金论	The Fund Theory
功能性货币	Functional Currency
汇兑损益	Exchange Gains or Losses
合并财务状况变动表	Consolidated Statement of Changes in Financial Position
换算损益	Translation Gains or Losses
举债经营收购	Leveraged Buyouts
母公司持股比例变动	Change in Ownership Percentage Held by Parent
交互分配法	Reciprocal Allocation Approach
货币项	Monetary Items
合伙清算	Partnership Liquidation
控股合并	Acquisition of Majority Interest
关税	Tariff
名义货币单位	Units of Nominal Currency
经营租赁	Operating Lease
流动性 / 非流动性法	Current/Non-current Method

Continued

Senior Accountant	
经济利润	Economic Income
破产受托人清算组会计	Trustee Accounting
联合会计报表	Combined Financial Statement
权益法	Equity Method
共同费用分配	Home Office-Branch Expense Allocation
货币 / 非货币法	Monetary/Non-monetary Method
利率期货交易	Interest Rate Futures Transaction
简单权益法	Simple Equity Method
汇率	Exchange Rate
母公司	Parent Company
红利法	Bonus Procedure
库藏股法	Treasury Stock Approach
劳务因素	Service Factor
精算报告	Actuarial Report
全面分摊法	Comprehensive Allocation
合并费用	Expenses Related to Combinations
间接标价法	Indirect Quotation
买入汇率	Buying Rate
期货合同	Futures Contract
混合合并	Conglomeration
控投公司	Holding Company
股票指数期货	Stock Index Futures
横向销售	Crosswise Sale
固定汇率	Fixed Rate
纳税影响法	Tax Effect Method
记账汇率	Recording Rate
横向合并	Horizontal Integration

Continued

Senior Accountant	
合并前股利	Pre-acquisition Dividends
可变现净值	Net Realizable
企业合并会计	Accounting for Business Combination
平仓盈亏	Offset Gain and Loss
卖出汇率	Selling Rate
金融期货交易	Financial Futures Transaction
会计利润	Accounting Income
合并损益表	Consolidated Income Statement
公允价值	Fair Value
期权	Options
间接控股	Indirect Holding
两笔交易观	Two-Transaction Opinion
企业合并	Business Combination
企业论	The Enterprise Theory
商业寄销	Consignment
权益理论	Equity Theory
融资租赁	Financing Lease
商品期货交易	Futures for Commodity
商誉法	Goodwill Procedure
生产能力保全	Maintaining Capital in Terms of Productive Capacity
额外费用	Premium
少数股东损益	Minority Interest Income
少数股东权益	Minority Stockholder's Interest
上市公告书	Listed Company Statement
剩余权益论	The Residual Equity Theory
时态法	Temporal Method
实体理论	Entity Theory

Continued

Senior Accountant	
实体论	The Entity Theory
受托人	Trustee
特定变动	Specific Change
所得税会计	Income Tax Accounting
所得税的跨期分摊	Inter-period Tax Allocation
税务会计	Tax Accounting
售后回租	Sale-Leaseback
个人所得税	Personal Income Tax
个人所得税报表	Personal Financial Statements
改组	Re-organization
改组计划	Re-organization Plan
复杂权益法	Complex Equity Method
附属公司	Associated Company
负权人偿金	Dividend
浮动汇率	Floating Rate
分支机构会计	Accounting for Branch
推定赎回损益	Constructive Gains and Losses on Bonds
推定赎回	Constructive Retirement
投机	Speculation
贴现	Discount
特定物价指数	Specific Price Index
分支机构	Branch
分期收款销货	Installment Sales
分次清算	Installment Liquidation
分部报告	Segmental Reporting
房地产收入	Real Estate Revenue
房地产成本	Cost of Real Estate

Continued

Senior Accountant	
房地产	Real Estate
多种汇率法	Multiply Exchange Rate Method
对境外实体的净投资	Net Investment in Foreign Entities
定量单位	Units of Measurement
递延法	Deferral Method
当代理论	Contemporary Theory
单一汇率法	Single Exchange Rate Method
退休金	Pension Plan
退休金会计	Accounting for Pension Plan
退休金给付义务	Pension Benefit Obligations
退休金成本净额	Net Periodic Pension Cost
退休基金资产	Pension Plan Assets
流转会计	Accounting for Circulation Tax
合伙权益的转让	Assignment of Partnership Interest
购买力损益	Purchasing Power Gains or Losses
非货币性项目	Non-monetary Items
单行合并	One-line Consolidation
外汇	Foreign Exchange
外币会计报表	Foreign Currency Statement
外币折算风险	Foreign Currency Translation Risk
外币统账法	Recording-Currency Method
外币投资风险	Foreign Currency Investment Risk
外币资产风险	Foreign Currency Assets Risk
外币会计报表折算	Translation of Foreign Currency Statements
外币兑换风险	Foreign Currency Exchange Risk
外币承诺	Foreign Currency Commitment
外币负债风险	Foreign Currency Liability Risk

Continued

Senior Accountant	
外币持有风险	Foreign Currency Holding Risk
外币分账法	Original-Currency Method
外币	Foreign Currency
外币业务	Foreign Currency Transaction
外币套期保值	Hedge
吸收合并	Merger
物价变动会计	Accounting for Price Changes
无偿债能力	Insolvency
完全合并	Full Consolidation
物价指数	Price Index
物价变动	Price Changes
完全应计法	Full Accrual Method
物价总指数	General Price Index
外汇期货交易	Foreign Exchange Futures Transaction
下推会计	Push-down Accounting
先折算后调整法	Transaction-re-measurement Method
现行成本 / 稳定货币会计	Current Cost/General Purchasing Power Accounting
现行成本	Current Cost
现行成本会计	Current Cost Accounting
先调整后折算法	Re-measurement-translation Method
销售代理处	Sales Agency
相互持股	Mutual Holdings
相对账户调节	Reconciliation of Home Office and Branch Accounts
新合伙人入伙	Admission of a New Partner
向上销售	Upstream Sale
衍生金融工具	Derivative Financial Instrument
销售式融资租赁	Sales-type Financing Lease

Continued

Senior Accountant	
向下销售	Downstream Sale
消费税	Consumer Tax
一笔交易观	One-transaction Opinion
业主权论	The Proprietorship Theory
一般物价水准会计	General Price Level Accounting
一般购买力单位	Units of General Purchasing Power
一般购买力保全	Maintaining Capital in Units of General Purchasing Power
印花税	Stamp Tax
应付税款法	Taxes Payable Method
营业亏损抵免	Operating Loss Carry-backs and Carry-forwards
以外币表示的应收款项或应付款项	Receivables of Payables Denominated in Foreign Currency
一次总付清算	Lump-sum Liquidation
营业税	Business Tax
永久性差异	Permanent Difference
原合伙人退伙	Retirement or Initial Partner
原始成本	Historical Cost
远期汇率	Forward Rate
时间性差异	Timing Difference
暂时性差异	Temporary Difference
增值表	Value Added Statement
债务重整	Debt Re-structuring
账面汇率	Recorded Rate
债权人会议	Committee Representation
直接融资租赁	Direct Financing Lease
直接标价法	Direct Quotation
直接控股	Direct Holdings
招股说明书	Prospectus

Continued

Senior Accountant	
中间汇率	Middle Rate
中期报告	Interim Reporting
重置成本	Replacement Cost
转租赁	Subleases
准改组	Quasi-re-organization
资本保全	Capital Maintenance
资本化价值	Capitalized Value
资本因素	Capital Factor
资产负债法	Asset Liability Method
存货转让价格	Inventory Transfer Price
创立合并	Consolidation
出租人会计	Accounting for Leases-lessor
持有	Holding Gains Losses
持仓盈亏	Opposition Gain and Loss
承租人会计	Accounting for Leases-lease
成本回收法	Cost Recovery Method
纵向合并	Vertical Integration
综合变动	General Change
子公司权益变动	Change in Ownership of a Subsidiary
子公司	Subsidiary Company
资源税	Resources Tax
成本法	Cost Method
财产信托会计	Fiduciary Accounting
财产税	Property Tax
部分分摊法	Partial Allocation
不合并子公司	Unconsolidated Subsidiaries
最低退休金负债	Minimum Liability

Continued

Senior Accountant	
租赁	Leases
租金	Rents
融资表	Off-balance-sheet Financing
比例合并	Proportionate Consolidation
保证金法	Deposit Method
资本资产定价模型	Capital Asset Pricing Model

Table 4: Cost Accounting Terms in Chinese and English

Cost Accounting	
Accounting terms in Chinese	Accounting terms in English
固定成本	Fixed Cost
直接人工成本差异	Direct Labor Variance
直接材料成本差异	Direct Material Variance
在产品计价	Work-in-process Costing
联产品成本计算	Joint Products Costing
生产成本汇总程序	Accumulation Process of Production Cost
制造费用差异	Manufacturing Expenses Variance
实际成本	Actual Cost
估计成本	Estimated Cost
工资费用分配	Salary Costs Allocation
成本曲线	Cost Curve
农业生产成本	Agriculture Production Cost
原始成本	Original Cost
重置成本	Replacement Cost
直接成本	Direct Cost

Continued

Cost Accounting	
间接成本	Indirect Cost
可控成本	Controllable Cost
制造费用分配	Manufacturing Expenses Allocation
理论成本	Theory Cost
应用成本	Practice Cost
辅助生产成本分配	Auxiliary Production Cost Allocation
成本控制程序	Procedure of Cost Control
成本记录	Cost Recorder
成本计算分批法	Job Costing Method
成本控制方法	Cost Control Method
生产费用要素	Elements of Production Expenses
历史成本	Historical Cost
未来成本	Future Cost
可避免成本	Avoidable Cost
不可避免成本	Unavoidable Cost
成本计算期	Cost Period
平均成本	Average Cost
个别成本	Individual Cost
社会成本	Society Cost
废品损失	Defective Work Losses
单位成本	Unit Cost
总成本	Total Cost
成本开支范围	Allowable Cost
成本转账	Cost Transfer
全面成本控制	Total Cost Control
商品销售成本	Cost of Merchandise Sold
价格差异	Price Variance

Continued

Cost Accounting	
存置成本	Holding Cost
已耗成本	Expired Cost
未耗成本	Unexpired Cost
相关成本	Relevant Cost
非相关成本	Irrelevant Cost
因素分析法	Factor Analysis Approach
目标成本	Target Cost
定额成本	Norm Cost
跨期摊提费用分配	Inter-period Expense Allocation
计划成本	Planned Cost
数量差异	Quantity Variance
燃料费用分配	Fuel Expenses Allocation
定额成本控制制度	Norm Cost Control System
定额管理	Management Norm
可递延成本	Deferrable Cost
不可递延成本	Non-deferrable Cost
成本控制标准	Standard of Cost Control
副产品成本计算	By-product Costing
责任成本	Responsibility Cost
生产损失核算	Production Loss Accounting
生产成本	Production Cost
预计成本	Predicted Cost
成本结构	Cost Structure
主要成本	Prime Cost
加工成本	Processing Cost
决策成本	Cost of Decision Method
在产品成本	Work-in-process Cost

Continued

Cost Accounting	
工厂成本	Factory Cost
成本考核	Cost Assess
制造费用	Manufacturing Expenses
动力费用分配	Power Expense Allocation
趋势分析法	Trend Analysis Approach
成本计算简单法	Simple Costing Method
责任成本层次	Levels of Responsibility Cost
对比分析法	Comparative Analysis Approach
产量比例法	Equivalent Units Method
原始记录	Original Record
可比产品成本分析	General Product Cost Analysis
预算成本	Budgeted Costs
销售成本	Cost of Goods Sold
停工损失	Loss on Work Stoppage
等级产品成本计算	Graded Product Costing
宏观经济成本	Macro-economic Cost
综合费用分配	Composite Expense Allocation
全部成本	Absorption Cost
商品采购成本	Merchandise Procurement Cost
成本考核目标	Cost Assessing Target
闲置成本	Idle Cost
账面成本	Cost of Book Value
再生产成本	Cost of Reproduction
增量成本	Incremental Cost
成本控制	Cost Control
成本流	Cost Flow
内部成本报表	Internal Cost Statement

Continued

Cost Accounting	
成本计算方法	Costing Method
成本计算对象	Costing Objective
成本计算单位	Costing Unit
成本计划管理体系	Planned Management System of Cost
成本计划	Cost Plan
成本会计	Cost Accounting
成本核算准则	Principle of Costing
成本核算程序	Cost Accounting Procedure
成本核算会计	Costing Account
成本核算	Costing
成本归集	Cost Accumulation
成本管理	Cost Management
成本分析	Cost Analysis
成本分配	Cost Allocation
成本分类账	Cost Ledger
成本分类	Cost Classification
成本调整	Cost Adjustment
初步报告	Costing Report
成本差异	Costing Variance
车间成本	Workshop Cost
厂内经济核算制度	Internal Business Accounting System
厂内结算价格	Internal Settlement Price
产品寿命周期成本	Product Life Cycle Cost
产品成本项目	Cost Items of Product
产品成本计划	Plan of Product Cost
产品成本	Product Cost
产成品成本	Finished Product Cost

Continued

Cost Accounting	
财务成本	Financial Cost
材料费用分配	Material Costs Allocation
不可控成本	Uncontrollable Cost
标准成本控制制度	Standard Cost Control System
标准成本	Standard Cost
比率分析法	Ration Analysis Approach
报告成本	Reporting Cost
半产品成本	Semi-finished Product Cost

Table 5: Management Accounting Terms in Chinese and English

Management Accounting	
Accounting terms in Chinese	Accounting terms in English
政治风险	Political Risk
再开票中心	Re-invoicing Center
现代管理会计专门方法	Special Methods of Modern Management Accounting
现代管理会计	Modern Management Accounting
提前支付	Leads
延期支付	Lags
跨国资本成本计算	Calculation of the Cost for Foreign Capital
跨国运转资本会计	Multinational Working Capital Management
跨国经营企业业绩评价	Multinational Performance Evaluation
经济风险管理	Managing Economic Exposure
交换风险管理	Managing Transaction Exposure
换算风险管理	Managing Translation Exposure
国际存货管理	International Inventory Management

Continued

Management Accounting	
股利转移	Dividend Remittances
公司内部贷款	Intercompany Loans
冻结资金转移	Repatriating Blocked Funds
冻结资金保值	Maintaining the Value of Blocked Funds
调整后的净现值	Adjusted Net Present Value

References

KESSLER M, ACOHIDO B. Data miners dig a little deeper [J]. USA Today, 2006-07-11.

BAKER S. Math will rock your world [J]. Business Week, 2006, 15: 54-62.

BUNN M. Taxonomy of buying decision approaches [J]. Journal of Marketing, 1993, 57: 38-56.

DOYLE R. Dressed for the occasion: font-product congruity in the perception of logotype [J]. Journal of Consumer Psychology, 2006, 16: 112.

DRUCKER P. Management: tasks, responsibilities, practices [M]. New York: Harper and Row, 1973.

FINE J. Marketing's drift away from media [J]. Business Week, 2009, 32: 64.

GORMLEY B. The U.S. government can be your lifelong customer [J]. Washington Business Journal, 2009, 57.

GROW B. Hispanic nation [J]. Business Week, 2004, 32: 58-70.

GRIMM M. Progressive Business [J]. Brandweek, 2005, 18: 16-26.

Keller L. The effects of brand name suggestiveness on advertising recall [J]. Journal of Marketing, 1998, 62: 48-57.

KOYLER P. Marketing: the underappreciated workhorse [J]. Market Leader Quarter, 2009, 2: 8-10.

LASSERE A. The marketing corner: marketing to African-American consumers [J]. Epoch Times, 2009, 12.

LEVITT T. Marketing myopia [J]. Harvard Business Review, 1960, 38: 50.

LOWERY M. Phonetic symbolism and brand name preference [J]. Journal of Consumer Research, 2007, 34: 406.

LOKEN B. Brand concept maps: a methodology for identifying brand association networks [J]. Journal of Marketing Research, 2006, 43: 549.

OZANNE U. Five dimensions of the industrial adoption process [J]. Journal of Marketing Research, 1971, 8: 322-328.

ZABIN J. The importance of being analytical [J]. Brandweek, 2006, 16: 21.